EDMUND WILSON
Our Neighbor from Talcottville

RICHARD HAUER COSTA

SYRACUSE UNIVERSITY PRESS
1980

"The Home Place," the title of the Introduction, is borrowed from a similar title, applied to a regional essay on Texas, used by Sid Cox, Department of English, Texas A&M University.

The poem "Palimpsest" is excerpted from *The House of Dust*, Book 4, Part 3, by Conrad Aiken, *Collected Poems* (New York: Oxford University Press, 1953), p. 185, and is reprinted by permission of Oxford University Press.

Photographs of Edmund Wilson were taken by F. Kurt Rolfes.

Library of Congress Cataloging in Publication Data

Costa, Richard Hauer.
  Edmund Wilson, our neighbor from Talcottville.

  (A York State book)
  Includes bibliographical references and index.
  1. Wilson, Edmund, 1895–1972. 2. Authors,
American—20th century—Biography. 3. New York
(State)—Biography. I. Title.
PS3545.I6245Z59   818'.52'09 [B]   80-23453
ISBN 0-8156-0163-8

For
Jo, who can't forget,
and Phil, who I hope will remember

Richard Hauer Costa was a Utica newspaperman when he first met Edmund Wilson. He is currently Executive Secretary of the South Central Modern Language Association and Professor of English at Texas A&M University. He has written critical studies of *H. G. Wells* (1967) and *Malcolm Lowry* (1972).

Contents

Acknowledgments

I am grateful to the late Elena Wilson for her permission to publish passages from her husband's many letters to me, 1962–72. Her encouragement at a critical point was vital.

For permission to use the photograph of the old house in Talcottville and to quote liberally from *Upstate*, I thank Edmund Wilson's dedicated publisher, Farrar, Straus & Giroux.

The evolvement of personal letters into a book manuscript took almost twenty years. My deepest appreciation of all goes to my friend of forty years, J. F. (Hop) Hopkins, the always responsive recipient of my letters about Edmund Wilson, and to my wife of thirty years, Jo. Both reversed my innately negative attitudes countless times about the possibility that a book would emerge.

I wish to thank a newspaperman colleague, Chuck Booth, for a special kindness that was *sine qua non*.

Thanks, too, are due David and Elaine Markson for keeping the faith over the long haul.

I am grateful to three of my graduate students—Pamela Lynn Palmer, Carlson Yost, and Tibbie Lynch—who read the complete manuscript in one or more of its three versions and made helpful criticisms.

Without a summer stipend from the College of Liberal Arts, Texas A&M University, in 1974, I might never have returned Upstate two years after Edmund's death; and without a recent

Texas A&M University Faculty Development Leave, I could not have completed this book. I wish it were possible to thank all the members of those committees.

Much thanks, in the final stage, goes to Laura Beall, who typed the manuscript.

RHC

Preface

*E*DMUND WILSON began spending his summers at the old house in 1951 "to get away from everything else." Throughout the 1950s he appears to have succeeded in family reunions, inducing "some of my long-absent cousins to join me" at the house he inherited from his mother. In the sixties, at the very time his disenchantment with America was most obsessive, a counter-movement was occurring within.

A loosely formed Upstate fraternity began building imperceptibly around the man whose authorial rebuffs of invaders had become legendary. There were no rules; you accepted the unstated—the necessary—terms. You didn't call; you waited to be called. You were always glad that you had waited.

My wife Jo and I knew Edmund as friends for almost the last decade of his life. As a native of Utica, Jo had strong regional interests; as an outsider, I had few. Our relationship with him therefore had variety and balance: literary and domestic. There was no need, after the first meeting, for gambits; everything by then was generated by his solicitude. The man *cared*. If we found a book we liked in common, he would be tireless, even with one already converted. If I could not interrupt his by-then-circumscribed reading with an enthusiasm of my own—and I never could—he would put me in touch with a sharer. Once a member of the benevolent order of

Wilsonians, you learned that his concern for your comfort meant everything, a preoccupation of his own distressed last years.

This memoir makes no pretense of being intimate. I was fortunate to share for brief periods toward the end of his life occasions that were marked by warm conversation. Although I never made it to Wellfleet, I cannot help but believe I should have viewed a more guarded Edmund Wilson, often deflected from the life he led "in the country" by the particular demands he must have felt as a showpiece of the Wellfleet literati, an elder in the international set of literary statesmen. Of course, anyone who knew him well also knows that the *essential* Wilson did not change with social geography. Still, Alfred Kazin's wartime picture of his neighbor on "Joan's Beach," that of an autocratic younger Wilson who was unable to make his escape from the oglers who guessed he was "someone" and maneuvered him against his will into gossip and polemic, provides a persona we saw much less frequently Upstate.[1]

I knew none of the immediate family well. I only saw the still striking-looking Elena Wilson twice—once at the old house and once in a large gathering. During most of the eight summers 1963–70, which form the basis of this memoir, she remained on Cape Cod. He preferred summers Upstate. Each honored the other's choice.

Whatever the value of this memoir, it rests with, depends on, the limitations. The Edmund Wilson I knew was off guard. Inaccessibly accessible in Talcottville and only occasionally obliged to perform as resident celebrity, he could fully apply himself to the effort of self-reformulation to which he was devoting himself in old age.

This book began as a series of letters to a close friend[2] with whom I have carried on a once-to-three-times-weekly correspondence since the end of World War II. That my epistolary monitor is a novelist who has savored nearly every word written by and about Wilson provided me, built in, with that perfect partner teachers of writing rightly advise neophytes to visualize as an audience. I was no neophyte when I began making full and prompt notes on all my encounters with Edmund and polishing them into informally substantive epistles. An Upstate newspaper columnist and reporter for many years before I became an academic, I had had professional experience in the faithful rendering of conversation. If I make no claim to a *verbatim* fidelity, I do claim trueness to the remembered *spirit*. I took no notes in Wilson's presence and would never have suggested the affront of a recording device. As soon after our conversations as I could get to it, I set down everything I could remember about them. Edmund Wilson's legendary command of the periodic sentence carried over into his talking style.

Perhaps my memory of the quality of the mind that, from the first, charged the hours in his company with vibrancy may have led me occasionally into over-feeling, perhaps over-writing. I trust not often. His life over, his books remain, a tribute to his extraordinary range of interests. But who that has known him can forget what Cyril Connolly called his "conversational double-take"?[3] "You agree, then, don't you, Edmund, that *Naked Lunch* is an important book?" "Oh—yes. What's that? Yes. . . . No. *No.* I don't agree." And then his chuckle, pitched to the decibels of near hysteria. "No, as a matter of fact, Burroughs is *terrible*. All that porn. No humor at all. Trashy."

The Home Place

"That river your old woman dreams about," I began, hoping to keep Rita there, "sounds like something in up-State New York." She looked up at me in her unaccountable quick, nervous, searching way: "Do you come from there?" she asked. "No," I said, "but I've been there a good deal."—Edmund Wilson, I Thought of Daisy (1929)

*L*IKE THOREAU, one of his heroes who came to know himself even as he "travelled a good deal in Concord," Edmund Wilson knew Upstate as spiritual true north since his childhood. The region captivated him. It was, by his own acknowledgment, the place where he felt the first intimations that, if he was not destined to become a poet, he would be "something of the kind."[1]

Upstate New York was the place, at the terminals of his life, he "felt excitement" summers fleeing urban Jersey for Talcottville, where there "is nothing between me and the widening pastures, the great boulders, the black and white cattle, the rivers, stony and thin, the lone elms like feather-dusters, the high air which sharpens all outlines, makes colors so breathtakingly vivid, in the clear light of late afternoon,"[2] and where, in old age, he returned summers, an international literary figure, but in Talcottville (pop. 80), a neighbor.

When, as was inevitable, the more compelling intellectual and social stimulations of prep school and college and travel fully rescued the teenage "Bunny" Wilson from Red Bank, they also left Talcottville and the "old stone house," for a long time, in the pale.

In an imperishable essay written in 1933, the thirty-eight-year-old newly hired staff critic on *The New Republic* writes of returning north, after many years away, on the Utica-to-Boonville milk train, seeking renewal and rebirth "up in the country." Instead, the journey he chronicles is to limbo, caught as he is between the Upstate worlds of the Bakers and the Talcotts—his maternal ancestors—and the making-it maelstrom of Manhattan and The Village which is inclining him, as it did his friend John Dos Passos, toward a vast leftward leap over his shadow.

The journey, of course, is one of place—to the old house, "one of the few of its kind among later wooden houses and towns, . . . an attempt to found a civilization . . . [blending] the amenities of the eastern seaboard with the rudeness and toughness of the new frontier"—and one of mind where he recognizes that, for him, Upstate and Talcottville are no less illusory than his recurrent dream of a gentle turning to a place of "wildness and freedom . . . of unalloyed delight."[3]

Talcottville has brought neither rebirth nor renewal, only depression. The return journey to the "old wooden booth . . . between First and Second Avenues" combines gloom with what he will years later identify, writing of Gogol, as the forces within which cause a man to be terrified of himself.[4]

During his misery, he reads anew of Lincoln, understands empathetically the identity agonies of the transplanted President: "the conscious focus of [the East's] terrible unconscious parturition."[5] For he cannot go back, any more than Lincoln, to the backwoods America of his ancestors. He cannot go forward either in a megalopolis of "sordid and unhealthy neighbors, who howl outside my window day and night." He ends the essay in the belief that he has left the old for a new in which he has not succeeded.

But go forward he does until he, too, "outlived the sons-of-bitches,"[6] universally recognized as America's Last Man of Letters. When, in his sixties, he returns Upstate for longer and longer visits, it is to an interior which is now all his own, a greenery of private universe which, as he had always known, lies squarely in the center of his head. Incapacitated as he is for bicycling, fishing, exploring, walking, and picnicking along Sugar River, which borders his property, he succumbs to what he calls an "old habit" but is actually a continuing "excavation" toward a final version of the renewal that was premature in his thirties.

Somebody else's genealogy is much like somebody else's vacation slides—largely uninteresting. I shall neither tax these pages with even a summary of what Wilson has done fully in the first seventy pages of his *Upstate: Records and Recollections of Northern New York* (1971) nor risk inevitable errors in so detailed a family tree. My omission should not undercut its importance to a man who could write that "there is all the difference between a place in which one feels the fibers of family and a place in which one is totally unaware of other peoples' similar fibers."[7]

I wonder, though, if any other major American writer, who was also a world traveller, turned as completely, at the end of a full and controversial literary life, to pastoral.

In his sixty-fifth year, he devotes a long diary entry to the job of "discovering" with Boonville friends a sylvan retreat at Dry Sugar River where he had picnicked many times as a youngster. And he—not unintentionally, I suspect—pairs the entry with a description of the verve with which he reads English memoirs of the late eighteen hundreds and early nineteen hundreds, the period in which he feels most at home.

He gives exactly twice as much space to the "Discovery of the Showy Ladyslipper" at age seventy as he gives to the "Death of Hemingway" four years before. To have even one of these rare June-blooming orchids is to hold a key to some secret place of the heart. No one of the blessed dares reveal where they grow naturally or how they got there even if the locales were known. Wilson uses the incidence of such a discovery for bucolic relief and mystery just as he uses the retired farmer and occasional chauffeur Albert Grubel, with his catalogue of holiday-accident deaths and gruesome suicides, for another kind of relief.

His extraordinary catholicity ranged over his country's literature until after World War II. For his final quarter-century he stopped caring about new American writers. He was learning Hungarian. The last time I saw him he observed with pride that, after six years of plodding, he had finished Macaulay's *History of England*. He continued to the end to concern himself with the great Russians, old and newer—Tolstoy, especially; émigrés of his own generation like Nabokov; younger ones like Solzhenitsyn, Mandelstam, Akhmatova; victims who survived but under extreme duress like Pasternak.

When Upstate, he had an Upstater's interests, some those of a gentryman—benevolently squirearchical—and some a regionalist's. On those occasions when he would take long drives with his amanuensis and *ezermester* (Hungarian for "master of a thousand arts") from West Leyden, Mary Pcolar, he often sought to satisfy his insatiable curiosity—about such as the origin of Sodom, New York, a village east of Speculator in a remote part of the Adirondacks; about the nature of the place, Palmyra, where Joseph Smith was supposed to have been visited by his angel. In Sodom, he met an old woman who told him that nothing was amiss in Sodom, but "what I call Gomorrah is down the road." Gomorrah proves to be a house whose new owner had allowed it to run down. At Palmyra, the self-described atheistical Wilson asked just the sort of question one would expect. What had happened to the Book of Mormon? The answer is part of a story Mary Pcolar recounted to me two years after his death (Chapter XVI).

Until angina ruled out walking, he went fishing with George Pcolar and attended the firemen's fair and parade mainly to see the Pcolar children perform.

Of special importance to the author of *Apologies to the Iroquois* (1960) were the tours of the Iroquois Confederacy with New York State Indian historian William N. Fenton, of Albany. He witnessed ceremonials at the Cattaraugus, Allegany, Tuscarora, and Onondaga reservations. Once he and I compared notes on a mini-Iroquois-nationalist movement on Schoharie Creek, near Amsterdam. A band of Mohawks pitched camp on some land which they claimed had been assigned to them by the United States in the Treaty of Fort Stanwix, 1784. For months they refused to leave. I covered the story for the Utica *Observer-Dispatch* in early October 1957, just missing by days Wilson's appearance at midmonth.

His final public appearance Upstate was at a symposium on the Iroquois, October 1968, when he shared the stage at Utica College with Fenton. He put on a false-face mask, carved by a Cayuga out of basswood and given him by an anthropologist friend. Edmund informed his audience that he had been assured the mask had not been blessed with magic powers and need not be kept covered for fear of its bringing a curse.

In a society where everybody appears obliged to accept transiency and with it the loss of old identity, persons like Edmund Wilson are inconceivable: cosmopolites who do go home again—and again.

While deeply interested in the Marxist revolution in his early years and in the Canadian separatist movement in his late, Wilson had understanding of, though limited sympathy for, individual "identity" difficulties. "I myself am well aware that although I embody different tendencies," he writes near the end of *Upstate*, ". . . I have never had much real doubt about who or what I was."

Certainty of who and what he was made the annual May-to-October pilgrimage *sine qua non*. I have a letter from Wellfleet, dated May 16, 1972, less than four weeks before his death, which reveals the priority he placed, even at his feeblest, on seeing the old house; if necessary, on dying in it. "I have had a slight stroke and can't talk clearly, but I hope to get up to Talcottville for the latter part of May and June."

He did.

PART ONE

Memoir

(1963–1970)

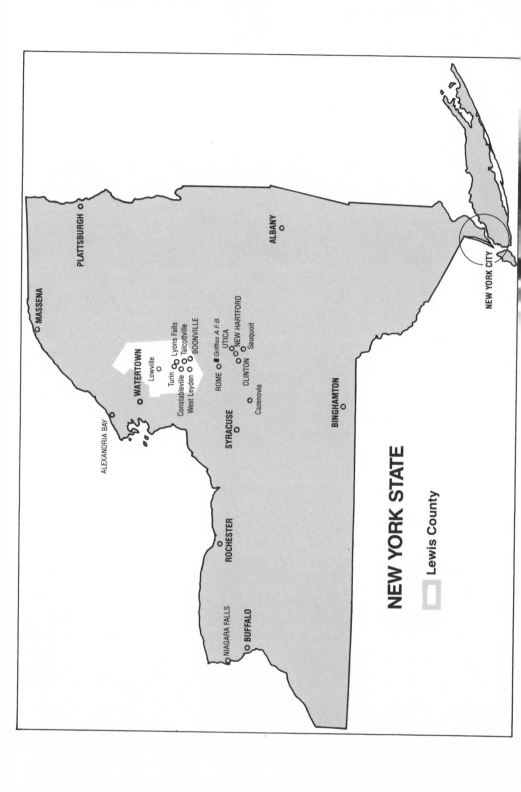

NEW YORK STATE

☐ Lewis County

Privilege of Rank

*B*EGINNING IN EARLY OCTOBER, the chill sets in swiftly, and Thanksgiving can be depended upon to be snowy. For an elderly party in his seventies, suffering from angina and the gout, any prospect of living alone in the old house was unthinkable. Compared to his principal residence, a house on Cape Cod at Wellfleet, Edmund Wilson's mother's home at Talcottville, New York, was conveniently remote, served only by air, or bus lines to the nearest large cities—Utica and Syracuse, forty and ninety miles distant—or by a determined driver.

If anything, I would find Talcottville's inaccessibility greater than Wilson's.

In the summer of 1961, having abandoned a fifteen-year career in newspaper journalism, I obtained an assistant professorship at the liberal arts branch of Syracuse University at Utica. I taught a split load in journalism, composition, and literature survey. Not yet knowing that most academics neither publish nor perish, I obtained a contract from Twayne Publishers, which had recently launched an English Authors Series to go with a flourishing United States Authors list, to do a book on H. G. Wells. Although I had been aware as a columnist-reporter for the Utica and Syracuse newspapers of Wilson's annual summer pilgrimage Upstate, I had been intimidated by his legendary brusqueness. Only once had I ventured straight north from Deerfield Corners on

Route 12, and that was on the insistence of a close friend who refused to conclude his visit without seeing where Edmund Wilson vacationed. We stopped for gas just past the old house. While an attendant filled the tank we looked at the rambling structure which at first glance looked more like an inn than a house.

This impression is quickly absorbed into another: a place built to last. The huge front porch, with two man-sized shuttered windows on either side of the door, was in full view to us, unenclosed but rendered formidable by eight white wooden columns which supported a white wooden balcony running along the second floor. The roof—source, I was to learn, of constant worry to its owner—came down over the balcony. Vines garlanded both porch and balcony; large ferns encroached on the porch; some sort of stone ornaments jutted in seeming disarray, unidentifiable from where we stood. Only a stone hitching-post made a utilitarian connection.

From that introduction I remember only one incident. Two teenage girls came running off the porch. One of them put her thumb to her nose and wiggled her fingers at us. Four years later, I learned that Helen, the only child of Wilson's marriage to Elena Mumm Thornton, fit perfectly the description of the girl who had thumbed her nose at us. She would have been fourteen.

A year after this tentative invasion, summer of 1962, I decided that the prospective authorship of a book on Wells conferred certain portfolio, even with Edmund Wilson. I wrote him a note asking if I might see him for a chat about Wells. Fully expecting a rebuff, one likely in the form of one of his postcard replies that began "Edmund Wilson regrets that it is impossible for him to . . . ," I was surprised to receive a typewritten note on *New Yorker* stationery but mailed from Talcottville: "I am sorry that I can't give you an interview—I am leaving here next Sunday. I don't like to give interviews anyway, unless I can play the *straight man* myself, as in the one you saw in *The New Yorker*." The note contained a postscript in longhand, something I took at the time (summer 1962) to be merely an afterthought: "I should like, though, to meet the people at Utica College."

Events through the sixties bore out the sincerity of that postscript.

Although accessible, Edmund Wilson was rarely interviewed, and his friends carried this a step further by refusing to

grant interviews *about* him without permission. These things I
learned from boning up on a profile, "Wilson," by Eleanor
Perenyi, carried in the July 1963 issue of *Esquire,* the only inter-
view-based article of substance that I had been able to find that
first year of my long wait. Wilson told me later that he granted the
Esquire interview only because Perenyi, the Baroness Palffi, an
American woman who had married European nobility, was a
friend. It is curious, then, that when I finally met Edmund Wilson
a year after his polite refusal, the occasion was an interview with
him—conducted by someone else.

Everybody knows that if you scratch a newspaper reporter
you find an aspiring novelist. The reporter, Chuck Booth, looked
like a studious college sophomore. At nineteen, he let it be known
that, like Hemingway, he was doing reporting only until he could
finish the novel in progress. Although he had read all of Hemingway's books, he never took to heart something Papa once said in
conversation. What you talk about you don't write.

One day, shortly after I had left newspaper work for the
classroom, Booth phoned. He had talked his managing editor into
starting a book page in the Sunday edition of *The Observer-
Dispatch.* He thought an interview with Edmund Wilson would be
in order. He had heard that I once tried unsuccessfully to meet
E.W. Now it was all set up. Would I care to join him for the
interview?

This was in late July 1963. I had just returned from examin-
ing the H. G. Wells special collection at the University of Illinois,
Urbana. I had even found in the voluminous files of Wells's correspondence the carbon copy of a note H.G.W. had written in 1932 to
Wilson, then a staff writer and reviewer for *The New Republic,* urging
him to read *The Work, Wealth and Happiness of Mankind.* Grateful
to Booth for the entry he was providing, I had no intention of stealing
his thunder with a barrage of questions on Wells. Perhaps, though,
one thing would lead to another.

Utica, almost the geographical center of New York State,
lies at the foothills of the Adirondacks. Although far less spectacu-
lar, it lies in the same relationship to its small mountains as—to
mention a French city I visited in 1959—Grenoble does to the
majestic *Alpes Maritimes.* I mention this likeness because it occurred to me four summers before when, upon awakening in the hotel

on the morning after a night arrival by bus from Paris, I was treated to an unforgettable scene: snow-capped mountains seemingly at the end of the avenue of our hotel. Utica, looking north, provides a version of this. New York State Highway 12, at Deerfield Corners, offers what in summer appears easy access to the North Country— to Boonville, its satellite village of Talcottville, and beyond to the Thousand Islands and the St. Lawrence. Deerfield Hill, especially the descent, has been the graveyard for many an unwary driver.

But now it was July, and during the thirty-five mile drive Chuck Booth drove with the easy concentration of one who had covered many stories in the region. He had hit on a way to launch the interview. He would take a page from Wilson's recent self-interview, which began, "What are you doing in London, Mr. Wilson?"[1] He would ask, "What are you doing in Talcottville, Mr. Wilson?" It seemed a good ploy, an ice-breaker that would at once show Wilson that Booth had actually read something of Wilson's and add a spark of levity.

Although I had driven to the old house a year ago, I trusted Chuck to know the way. We missed 12-D at Boonville, a kind of "frontage" road to 12 and the only way to reach Talcottville. We were well on our way toward Watertown before realizing our mistake. When the house finally came in view we were fifteen minutes late for our three o'clock appointment. Chuck opened the screen door and sounded the doorbell. A portly gentleman wearing a white shirt, open at the neck, and white sneakers appeared. "Wuh-wuh-won't you come in, Mr. Booth," he said. Edmund Wilson looked dramatically smaller—less forbidding—than I had expected. He shuffled his way into a room on the right. Looking back on our ten-year acquaintance, I almost never remember the man *walking*. He shuffled. He bid us sit down. "What are you doing in Talcottville, Mr. Wilson?" The question hung in the air. Wilson began, almost non-stop, talking about his grandfather, the single son among eight Baker daughters who were reared in the house.

While he rattled off Talcottville history to Chuck Booth, who pretended to take notes, I had a chance to study Edmund Wilson. He was, like me, a *pyknic*, short and stocky, inclined to be heavy. I got no sense of the severity of the face which came across in every likeness I had ever seen of him. Rather, as Eleanor Perenyi was perhaps the first to point out, he was Pickwickian. The voice was of a high timbre, cultivated, and given to an almost imperceptible stutter. He laughed easily but never robustly and was having trouble crossing one leg over the other. He juggled things between his fingers but not, as I would learn, for Captain Queeg–like reasons. He took to shuffling a deck of cards.

The old stone house had to be a large one in the early nineteenth century, he informed us, because of the necessity of lodging many people. The place was a town in itself—hostelry, town hall, social center, source of supplies. "Here in this house," he said, making no attempt to conceal his gentryman's pride, "was where my ancestors set up the boundary between Oneida and Lewis counties, and *there*," pointing to a china closet in the dining-room, "was the Talcottville post office." He had to bring to mind the year of George Washington's death because there had been a meeting, likely its first, in the house on that occasion. Unable to remember whether the year was 1799 or 1801, Wilson rose from his chair to look it up. 1799.

Although I kept silent, in line with my resolve, I wondered how Chuck would get Wilson off the subject of Talcottville and the family tree.

Had Wilson seen a recent reassessment of his novel, *I Thought of Daisy*, in which the critic, whom Chuck did not name, termed the book, originally published in 1929, a truer transcript of the twenties than *The Great Gatsby*?

"Those things don't mean anything to me," he said, an edge creeping into his voice. "*Gatsby* is simply a better novel." There was a pause, but not the kind a speaker observes when he wants the full impact of something to sink in. "Have either of you read *Memoirs of Hecate County*?" We hadn't. "I've always thought that novel as rather neglected by the critics."

Although he had not read Wilson's once-banned *Hecate County*, Booth had done enough homework to pronounce it *Hecat-y* and to have read an early review or two. "But is it *really* a novel?" He simply released the implicitly critical words in the manner of a Ph.D. oral. I had to admire his courage. "Diana Trilling considered it a volume of short stories."[2]

"It's a novel, of course," Wilson snapped. "At least Malcolm Cowley recognized its affinity with *Winesburg, Ohio*."[3]

What did he think of William Faulkner's surprising ranking

of Thomas Wolfe as our best contemporary novelist—he tried for more than the others—and Hemingway, who tried for much less, well down the list?[4] When Wilson shook his head without replying, Booth asked him, since he had known both writers so well, "did he consider Fitzgerald or Hemingway the better novelist?"

"I have no idea about things like that," Wilson replied. "What difference would it make, whatever I said?"

When Chuck persisted with other questions of the is-so-and-so-a-better-writer-than-so-and-so? Wilson parried them by asking his questioner how *he* felt about it. Asked about the quality of TV writing, he said he never watched television except "a couple of J. F. Kennedy press conferences, the McCarthy hearings, a few things like that." He had never heard of Rod Serling, had read nothing by Norman Mailer, and thought that *The Hundred-Dollar Misunderstanding* was "promising." He thought that James Baldwin was the best black writer he had read "because when you read him you forget he's black." Time after time Booth would ask him about a modern American writer—Vonnegut, Bellow, Barth—and Wilson would say, almost with alacrity, that he had read nothing by the writer. "I'm rereading Macaulay's *History of England* after thirty years," he said. "I'm reading the books I missed and rereading all the neglected minor Edwardians that I enjoyed in college."

Accustomed to the conversation of academics, where one-upsmanship is the name of the game and one never dares let a colleague know one hasn't read the book that was all the rage, I found in Edmund Wilson's candor a seeming humility for which I was unprepared. Later, however, from the vantage of a decade's friendship, I came to recognize Wilson's admissions of ignorance as evidence of the privilege of rank, the kind of assurance that puts the position-jockey, who namedrops books and authors, on notice that he won't stoop to be competitive.

Name-labels having failed as gambits, Booth sought entry into some sort of cultist terrain: the agony of the literary artist, for example. Why, he asked, did Edmund Wilson think that Oscar Wilde, Scott Fitzgerald, Hemingway, Hart Crane, Dylan Thomas all came to bad ends?

"If you mean why were their endings so dismal after early promise, that theory simply won't do. Did you know that a number of Wilde's books are built around the idea of a man who looks fine on the outside but has this hidden thing—*Dorian Gray*, and so forth? Wilde, as we know, was in the final stages of syphilis when he died. He'd known he had it at Oxford, thought he'd got rid of it when he got married, and then learned after his marriage that he still had it. I'm sure that knowledge contributed to his problem.

"I've always felt that Hemingway was just this side of sanity for a great many years. I talked to a psychiatrist recently who took the view that the Mayo Clinic ruined him. They gave him shock treatments, you know. When he came out of the clinic he was a different person."

Until that moment I had remained silent. Booth had had his chance. ·I asked Wilson if he had read an article in *Partisan Review*,[5] published a few months after Hemingway's suicide, in which Leslie Fiedler describes a journey from Montana State University to Hemingway's final retreat at Ketchum, Idaho. The essay, despite Fiedler's expressed admiration, made Hemingway to be senile, dotty.

"It was cruel to take such relish in destroying what was left of Hemingway's masculine image," Wilson said.

I pointed out that Maugham was still going strong at ninety.

"Yes, the old scoundrel," blurted out Wilson. "That sort of writer goes on forever."

I then told Wilson that I had interviewed Maugham at his villa at Cap Ferrat in 1959,[6] that I had found him congenial, and that my opportunity came on the basis of a newspaper column in which I had written that he was the only writer I could read while riding on the New York Central.

"I can't read him *anywhere*," Wilson retorted, his voice rising to honor the perfect squelch.

"Maugham appeared to be taking Max Beerbohm's death rather hard when I saw him," I offered.

"They weren't close friends, you know," said Wilson. "I went to Rapallo with Sam Behrman several years before Max's death. Max would say, 'You know what I tell everyone who comes here? Ah yes, you've been to Maugham on your way to Berenson.' Max couldn't do Maugham's portrait and thought it was because he didn't like his face.[7] I always thought Max looked like

Bismarck. When I expressed this to Max, he brought out a self-portrait striking a Bismarck pose."

I was trying to get Wilson to say something favorable about Maugham, long a favorite of mine, and reminded him of the hatchet job he once did on Louis Bromfield. Surely he rated Maugham above Bromfield. Ought he to have judged Maugham in a *New Yorker*[8] review on the basis of *Then and Now*, a potboiler W.S.M. wrote to make money during a period of low financial ebb and the only Maugham book he had dealt with at any length? Surely he could appreciate the devastation Maugham had wrought on Hugh Walpole when he lampooned Walpole in the characterization of the opportunistic Alroy Kear in *Cakes and Ale*.

"That may be," he replied, "but the rest of the novel is so awful. Walpole was insufferable, no doubt of that. Henry James said good things about him only because he liked young writers to sit at his feet and *cher maître* him. James knew Walpole was second-rate."[9] Wilson had deftly shifted the stress from Maugham, about whom he obviously did not wish to talk, to Walpole and James, about whom he did. It was a diversionary tactic I was to observe in him many times.

At least we were on the Edwardians. I was fairly certain that Wilson did not recall either my name or the original request of a year ago for a chat about H. G. Wells. I asked him if he knew Anthony West. He said he did but that I was never to quote him "on anything about Anthony West." But he sped into the topic anyway. "His predicament has been hard on him, being the illegitimate son of Rebecca West and Wells. She must be a holy terror. You know, of course, that West's novel about the whole thing—*Heritage*—has never been published in England. And that he will never be able to write a thing about his father, at least in England, while his mother is still alive. Apparently, for all the litigation, she never got over loving Wells.[10]

"Even Wells's legitimate children made it hard for West to live in England. It's well-known over there that three or four other Wells offspring are kicking about, fortunately none so famous as Anthony West."

It may have been at this first meeting—more likely at a subsequent, more relaxed time—that Wilson told a story, which he attributed to Elinor Wylie, touching on Wellsian passades that led to pregnancies. Miss Wylie was in the hospital when a nurse informed her that the great man was visiting an obstetrical patient in a room nearby. Thus the young poet had a peek at one of the most famous writers in the world in characteristic setting. At another time, after several highballs, Wilson took off on a famous phrase originated by Wells. He observed that during Wells's Fabian phase the members warned their suffragette daughters to have nothing to do with Bertie Wells lest they become the shape of things to come.

Wilson took us through the old house. The one feature that I, who have no feeling for houses, ancestral or otherwise, reserved for later comment to Jo, was the window panes upstairs on which famous visitors had written, with crystal pen, their poems—Stephen Spender, the opening lines of *I Think Continually of Those Who Were Truly Great*, W. H. Auden, Dorothy Parker ("we were pretty high; I doubted she could write anything"), Nabokov, in Russian ("he's absolutely the opposite kind of man from his character Pnin"[11]), his old Princeton mentor Christian Gauss, many others.

He served Molson's Canadian ale. We had already drunk three bottles each when he surprised us by moving to the door and motioning for Chuck and me to follow. We were to drive him to Boonville to refill his cabinet with the Molson's.

It would be later in our relationship that I would come to take for granted that, in Boonville anyway, Edmund Wilson could walk down Main Street without anyone noticing him. Occasionally, to be sure, someone would nod or say hello, to which Wilson always responded, frequently by first name. By now it was drawing on six o'clock, dinnertime, and Main was crowded. We entered a small grocery store. Wilson walked knowingly to the ice compartment and picked out six bottles, hesitating when he noticed that he had got some American beer mixed in. These bottles he replaced with Molson's. Chuck paid the bill, but Wilson reached into his wallet anyway. When Booth, standing next to him in front of the cashier, told him he had already paid, Wilson looked surprised. "Oh, I didn't recognize you."

Back at the house we drank another round and then repaired to his workroom. My eyes fastened on an imitation log with a dictionary on it; a file case labelled *Dead Sea Scrolls*, the book he would tell us he was bringing up to date; bookshelves full of paperbacks in French and English. He had just returned from Canada, from Toronto, "a country where perfectly astounding things are happening in the culture." He was writing, he said, a long article on Canada for *The New Yorker*.[12] By his kind of journalistic transplantation, it and related writings would become a book. Wilson held up two veteran novelists of British Canada for special praise— Hugh MacLennan and, apparently an article of faith with him, Morley Callaghan. "Have you read Morley Callaghan?" he shot at us, without waiting for an answer (we hadn't, anyway). "I've been an admirer of his for forty years. Don't miss his new book, nonfiction, *That Summer in Paris*. I've just reviewed it in *The New Yorker*. Morley has the gift of moral objectivity so that when he writes about the unpleasant traits in Hemingway and Fitzgerald he never indulges in malice. By the way, I'm about to be flogged by Mary Hemingway for some comments I made about her husband in that review."[13]

As to the writers of French Canada, he was especially taken with André Langevin and a young woman from Quebec, later to be his neighbor in Wellfleet, Marie-Claire Blais. He expressed regret that he would be unable to finish the piece on Canada before leaving for Europe in September. His Canadian library would go with him. He planned to place his teenage daughter Helen in a Swiss school and contemplated setting up residence there himself. He said he was taking up Hungarian—said it with no more amplification than that several of his little-known plays had been translated into Hungarian and were being performed in Budapest.

He showed us a collection of magic gimmicks on his shelves. "It's my only hobby. I've done magic since I was a boy." He spoke admiringly of Houdini whom he had known personally. Then he performed a rather amazing card trick. He had me cut the deck, hand the two halves to him, and then select three cards from the top. I held them. Wilson walked to a desk, bade me follow, and the first two cards that slowly rose were identical to the first two in my hand. The third one wouldn't rise, kept falling back. Wilson showed—feigned?—chagrin, finally got the third card to rise. It did not match the third card in my hand. Then the climax: somehow of its own accord the wrong card turned over to become the right one. "You see to what depths I've fallen as a magician," he said.

We talked about *The New Yorker,* to which I have sub-
scribed for thirty years. I brought up an old gripe. My favorite
postwar novel in English is *Under the Volcano* by Malcolm Lowry.
The New Yorker, in one of its devastating capsule reviews, dismissed *Volcano* as a "rather good imitation of an important novel."[14]
Fifteen years later, in another capsule review, this time of a posthumous collection of short fiction by Lowry, *Volcano* was called a
masterpiece.[15] How could such disparate notices happen? Wilson,
without hesitation: "Bill Shawn and Harold Ross before him devoted great energy to the lead review, but the smaller ones are
often dishonest." He said he only goes to New York two or three
times a year and hardly knows anybody on the magazine anymore.
Unlike *Vanity Fair,* where he worked briefly in 1920 before joining
New Republic, members of *New Yorker* do not as a rule know one
another. "Sid" (S. J.) Perelman was one of the few he knew and
liked. Mention of Perelman reminded him of a story. The humorist
had visited Hemingway in Italy the later years. Wilson asked
Perelman how Hemingway looked. "Wonderful, and the talk was
great except when he conversed about war, Spain, the bullfights."
Thurber was a burned-out case, Wilson reported. Blindness had
brought on drinking, and the drinking brought on barrages of insults that made the humorist unrecognizable to anyone who knew
him in better days.

Talk of Thurber brought on talk about the Algonquin.
Booth asked if Wilson had ever been an Algonquin round-tabler. "I
was invited a number of times, but I rarely went. My God, who
would want to sit around with that crowd."

The benevolent Wilson that emerges from Perenyi's profile
assumed the literary world was well acquainted with the "other"
Wilson. As, I was to learn, he did with everything that was ever
written about him, Wilson expressed displeasure over the latest.
The most complimentary things I would ever hear from him about
books and articles on himself were of the it's-not-altogether-bad-is-
it? variety—his exact words on Sherman Paul's *Edmund Wilson,*
published by the University of Illinois Press in 1965, two years
after our first conversation. Once, in a letter to his Upstate amanuensis, Mary Pcolar,[16] he expressed grudging acceptance of a review because the reviewer "at least appears to have read the
book." Now he declined to show appreciation of a piece of personal

publicity most authors would sell their souls for, in a national magazine which would later name him one of the one hundred most important men in the world. For one thing, the article made him out to be inaccessible ("I'm always accessible") and an "intellectual" ("there was no such nonsense about being an 'intellectual' when I was in college. We all enjoyed literature and ideas; that was all there was to it").

By now it was heading on seven o'clock. I suggested that he let Chuck and me take him to dinner. At first he demurred. In a few minutes he had worked out an arrangement. He would accompany us only if we would let him suggest the place and pay the bill. We agreed to split the check. His suggestion was the Towpath Lodge, fewer than ten miles due north in the Village of Turin. The owners, the Heusers, were close friends of his. The place does a huge business during the long ski season Upstate, and a certain Swiss atmosphere is sought, he explained during the short drive. Klaus Heuser, however, is the son of a German chemist, his wife Mignonne a French Canadian from Montreal. Wilson promised us a kind of continental atmosphere one would not have thought possible in the country.

As we entered it became immediately obvious that the literary celebrity had been expected. I had the impression some set piece was being re-enacted for his benefit. Klaus Heuser, who walked with a decided impairment, limped toward us to greet Wilson. "How are you, Mr. Wilson?" Introductions were made as he seated us near the bar. There were only two customers at the bar; I was aware that everyone was talking so as to reach the last row of the balcony. A lovely woman, late thirtyish, moved quickly from behind the bar to greet Wilson. Mignonne Heuser changed in a flash the tempo from the servile to the intimate. "We enjoyed the profile in *Esquire* but not the picture—*so severe*," she said. "You're not like that at all, Mr. Wilson." A coquette would have phrased the comment as a question. Her French accent would have been effective, in that way, if she had said, "*You* are not like *that*, are you, Mr. Wilson?" Phrasing her words clearly as a tribute, Mignonne put Wilson at ease. And, unwittingly, she had clinched a point about Edmund Wilson. None of his published photographs looked like the Upstate squire I was coming to know. Another matter, faintly paradoxical. At the Towpath, Wilson clearly warmed to being the focus of attention. He enjoyed the attention—enjoyed it because it was neighborly, because it was non-literary, because it did not call for a Wilsonian catechism.

Once the flow of trade resettled itself without a focus, Wilson turned his attention to the Heusers' blonde daughter, a teenager and, like her mother, lovely. "H-h-how are you, *cherie?*" he asked in a way that I recall as impressively unmagisterial, the sort of voice of which the impostor in the *Esquire* portrait would be incapable. I did not then know that the youngster he called *cherie*—actual name Monique—was about the same age as his own daughter Helen.

I shall have more to say, in sequence, about the paternal Edmund Wilson. His warm exuberance with Monique Heuser that day at the Towpath was nothing like the perfunctory attention adults often give to the youngsters of friends. I am now persuaded to believe that even the sight of another teenager put him in mind of Helen, whom I was to meet only once. In his last years the compulsion to be a good father in his last chance must have been overwhelming. Hermann Hesse writes in *Steppenwolf* about the twin compulsions of his protagonist to be a good burgher *and* a wolf of the steppes. Wilson's final years may have been spent in resolving just such a split. His "adoption" of Mary Pcolar, I would learn from her, was Pygmalion *and* paternal. He who had let *them* down in their youth was now himself being let down by the grown children of his old age.[17]

I may have been turning over thoughts like these as we drove back to the old house. Chuck did most of the talking. What did Wilson think of John Dos Passos and *U.S.A.?* Once again, he replied by turning Booth's question back on him. What did *he* think of Dos Passos and *U.S.A.?* Chuck proceeded to give the trilogy his characteristic Greatest American Novel treatment. Wilson, hearing the unqualified panegyric, half assented, then half backed off, with the conversational "double-take" treatment I was to hear often during the next decade ("Oh—yes. What's that? Yes . . . No. *No*. I don't agree. . . ."). When Chuck let up on the questions, Wilson began to speak movingly of his old friend whose Marxian phase had preceded his own but also had petered out sooner. What we heard that evening was another—this one unwritten—wound-and-bow analysis. Dos Passos was illegitimate, a fact which Wilson believed produced the leftist strain of the early novels. "He had to go to court to claim extensive property in Virginia belonging to the family which sired him. Once he became a landowner, he appears to have gone the other way: far to the right. Unprecedented, really."

As my first meeting with Edmund Wilson drew to a close, he mentioned for the first time a Hungarian-American woman who had been acting as his secretary and chauffeur throughout the summer. If he gave her name, I did not note it. She was, of course, Mary Horbach Pcolar. She was also helping him to master Hungarian, which he was determined to have join Hebrew and Russian as languages of which he had lately acquired a reading knowledge on his own.

Wilson, incidentally, paid the check at the Towpath except for the tip. He promised to allow Booth and me to reciprocate in Utica. We set a date for two weeks. He walked to the car with us. If was after ten o'clock. We had been with him more than seven hours.

II

Serenade and Sendoff

*T*HE PHONE RANG in the middle of the afternoon on a Saturday eleven days after the interview at the old house. I had dozed off over the TV baseball game-of-the-week; I barely heard the tinkle downstairs. I waited to decode my wife's telephone ritual. If Jo's voice sounded formal, even forbidding, it would be one of my students; if puzzled, it would be someone with a news tip, forgetting that I had left the newspaper two years ago; if deliberately colloquial, it would be one of her sisters. Jo's voice on this occasion sounded restrained; I could not calibrate it.

A pause. Her footfalls on the stairs from the kitchen to the TV room. "It's Edmund Wilson," she said.

I could not conceive of talking to Edmund Wilson on the telephone. I had held no illusions that he would keep his promise to get in touch in two weeks.

"Hello."

"Heh-heh-hello. Costa? This is Edmund Wilson. Can you come here for a drink? I'm ah-ah-at the Fort Schuyler Club."

The high-pitched voice sounded cranky though not necessarily at any human antagonist. I had the impression of someone disciplining a gadget that wouldn't mind. There was a problem. Would I be responsible for driving him back up Deerfield Hill? He had already phoned Chuck Booth at *The Observer-Dispatch*. He would be joining us at the Fort Schuyler. Wilson rang off without saying goodbye. He had made the gadget mind.

When I called to Jo, shouting something about Edmund Wilson wanting to see me, her single question brought me back to earth. Was Wilson, who did not drive, merely bargaining for a chauffeur?

It was arranged that Chuck and I were to meet him at the Fort Schuyler at five, the phone call having come at two. I arrived first and spotted Wilson reading a newspaper—no doubt the *Watertown Times*, the only Upstate paper he ever read—in the lounge. He suggested we adjourn immediately to the bar—vacant, as it turned out, except for us. He had already had a vodka martini. He ordered two more. I asked him if he would join Jo and me for dinner at our house. He agreed without hesitation. I phoned Jo that, including Booth, we would have dinner for five, the fifth being Phil, our son, who had just turned eight. In that way she has, Jo had anticipated Wilson's coming and dispatched Phil to his grandfather's.

We arrived in two cars, Wilson driving with Chuck, and all three of us, as the saying goes, feeling no pain. At their introduction, Wilson kissed Jo's hand. She responded by bringing out what we needed least, a bucket of martinis. Hers were only 2½ to 1. Not even the knowledge that I would be driving eighty miles, and with a world figure, slowed me down.

Looking back over the eight summers, 1963–70—the Wilson Years—I realize how fully the first two meetings set the invariable pattern. There would always be more drinking than dining. In fact, I cannot recall Wilson ever enjoying food. At a restaurant, chicken livers was a feast. Jo learned to serve soup with meatballs, bite size. I soon found out why. He had had to give up most meat dishes in deference to his dentures. There would always be the appointment with his dentist and never less than an urgency about it.

Wilson nibbled at his salad while drinking glass after glass of burgundy. He explained that, with a weight problem and a heart condition, he could not eat *and* drink. That and the denture business made the serving of a thick sirloin a tactical blunder.

Conversation missed the mark, too; nothing like the high

standard of eleven days ago at the old house. Drink rendered him inarticulate. The slurring of words gave way to the characteristic stutter, almost pleasant to hear under ordinary circumstances, but now paralyzing, tortured. What talk he managed was mainly about his current *New Yorker* essay on Boris Pasternak, the man's courageous and willed duality. Wilson said that he was not at all put off by Pasternak's remark to a *Nation* interviewer that *Dr. Zhivago* should not be read to contain religious symbolism as he (Wilson) was going to great lengths to demonstrate. It was a part of Pasternak's ordeal that he had continually to make one sort of statement publicly. The public sentiments were never the real Pasternak. He cited correspondence between Pasternak and his Italian publisher Feltrinelli: cablegrams which, on the one hand, ordered the publisher to drop plans for *Zhivago* but were followed by communications *sub rosa* which asked if the publisher had understood that the initial ones were sent to satisfy the commissars and were, of course, to be ignored.[1]

I was learning early in our friendship that Edmund Wilson, always scrupulously careful never to repeat a story, could be led to restate the gist of material that he had already published. The Pasternak theory had appeared more than four years ago in *The Nation* and, expanded, in *The Bit Between My Teeth*. Later I would hear from his lips compressed versions of his *Wound and the Bow* essays on Kipling and Dickens.

P. G. Wodehouse has a story about a chronic stammerer who experienced no trouble singing. Just when it appeared that we would have nothing to remember about the first time Edmund Wilson was a guest in our house, he asked Jo her maiden name. Always fond of telling new friends that her full name is *Maria Giuseppa Dolores Basilio Costa,* four iambs concluding with a single trochee—Mar-*ee*-yah Jew-*zeph*-ah Do-*loh*-res Bah-*see*-lio *Coh*-stah—no sooner had she made it through the exaggerated phonetics than Wilson began using his voice, at its highest register, for another purpose altogether. He began to sing:

> Oi, Mari! Oi, Mari!
> Quanta suonn aggie pierze
> ie pe te;
> famm' addurnu
> almen ua notte abbracciate cu to . . .[2]

Using his unused steak knife as a baton, Wilson sang while we three did our best to follow. So charged were Jo and I with this comic non sequitur that neither of us asked then, or at any time during the next decade, how it was that he knew the words. And not just some words but all of them—and in Neapolitan dialect![3] Had he been sober, could he have called them to mind?

When it grew dark we moved from the patio, where Jo had set a sumptuous table, to the family room. Wilson shuffled slowly to a chair. The one he occupied was a favorite of our brown cocker spaniel. "Caesar" gave up the place reluctantly, and Wilson bent to pet him. "Good old dawg!" he said. Having nothing to do with the fame of the man who spoke them, the memory of those words has always stood to me as the essence of benevolence, even goodness. I have remembered them more often than most of the weightier ones.

It was time to make good my pledge to drive him home. Chuck volunteered, but I would not be denied, tired as I was. Chuck, working the day shift, had to be up early.

My driving has never been such as to instill confidence, but I made every effort to proceed under 35 m.p.h. toward the North Country. The man in the ratty old hat and raincoat gripped the arm of his seat. There was no conversation, not even intersecting monologues. Was it the driving or the drinks? I thought of a pun Malcolm Lowry had stolen from his mentor Conrad Aiken: *introverted coma*. Edmund Wilson seemed lost in an introverted coma.

We must have driven halfway when, breaking a long silence, Wilson asked if we might stop. We had come to a tavern, a welcome patch of neon to break up the somberness inside and outside the car. I assumed he wanted another drink. He struggled out of the car, shuffled toward the side of the tavern, stopped. In the full glare of the neon sign, Edmund Wilson stood by the side of Route 12 relieving himself. I followed suit.

Who knows by what chemistry of give-and-take, trial-and-error, the mind-consciousness of awe becomes the blood-consciousness of friendship? Was the transition begun that Saturday night, halfway to the old stone house, when we stood together, defenses down, by the side of the road?

When we were moving again, he became suddenly talkative, solicitously so—on Wells. "There's a scene in either *Marriage* or *The New Machiavelli* . . . Scott Fitzgerald admired Wells tremendously. I'd got him to read Wells as a kind of halfway point from Booth Tarkington to somebody really good. . . . In *Gatsby* you remember the scene with all the fashionable parasites on Gatsby's lawn. . . . The one in which Nick Carroway ticks off all the names. . . . Scott modelled that scene on one in Wells. . . . Too much to drink to remember. . . . Will look it up when I get back to Wellfleet. . . ."

And moments later: "Do young people still read Wells's scientific romances? My son Reuel is a science-fiction enthusiast. Doesn't think much of Wells. But those early short stories. . . . Came on them first at the Hill School. You have, of course, read the collection *Twelve Stories and a Dream*. The final story, 'A Dream of Armageddon,' unforgettable. . . ." He began quoting the last lines: "'Nightmares,' he cried: 'nightmares, indeed! My God! Great birds that fought and tore.'"

Returning to Utica, I wondered how many years it had been since he had called to mind the last lines of a story from his teens. Was it merely the drinking that had liberated them after perhaps a half-century's solitary confinement in memory? And the perfect recall of *Oi, Mari*? And would he, tomorrow, remember that he had remembered?

We did not have to wait long for the telephone to ring and to hear that cantankerous voice. Could we pick him up at the old house on Sunday a week, August 29, around 5:30, and join him for dinner at the Towpath? I had raved to Jo about the Heusers, the continental flavor deep in the country, the chance to see Edmund Wilson at his best.

No date with him ever started so awkwardly. We arrived, for once, precisely on time. He was waiting on the porch. As we walked up the path, another car drew up behind mine. No sooner were we inside the door than the bell sounded. A flustered Wilson ushered a man into the vestibule. His age appeared vaguely between mine, forty-two, and Wilson's, sixty-eight. He wore a leather jacket over a lumberjack shirt. His face was familiar in that vague way which is attributable to a kind of spontaneous "typing"—too slim to be the Upstate woodsman his jacket formulated him as—rather, perhaps, a farmer? Wilson, not one to manage unexpected introductions gracefully, clearly was finding himself in a predicament. "Wha—wha—what did you say your name was?" He flung the question in my direction. "This is Wah-Wah-Walter Edmonds. Walter, meet Mr. and Mrs. Costa from Utica." He had come by to pick up a volume of his short stories, *Mostly Canallers*. It was well known that Edmonds, unlike Wilson a native of the North Country, maintained an estate in Boonville. He apologized for having to rush off; said goodbye to the older writer; wished him a pleasant journey to Wellfleet in three days and *bon voyage* to Switzerland after Labor Day.

"I like Edmonds, but I can't read his novels," Wilson began even before the subject of his critique had driven off. Grace Root urged me to read the book.[4] I must admit that these stories are better than the novels. In his long fiction, none of the characters come through at all. He's something of a permanent writer of juveniles, but in several of the *Canallers* stories there are touches of the gothic, incidents of a kind of pathological nature. All surprising in Edmonds."

When we sat down in the livingroom, the conversation turned to Wells. "Have you worked through the whole of Wells? I must say that I'm partial to the Edwardians. I keep a shelf of Edwardian fiction by my bed. It's surprising to find another enthusiast in anyone of your generation, unless you are older than you look. I've been reading Shaw and Beerbohm. I don't go back to Wells any more, but I read all of his books when I was younger. There was—what?—an exhilaration in the early things he almost entirely lost. Occasionally it appears momentarily. Parts of *The Outline of History*, a work I don't think much of, show some of the spirit of those early stories."

I asked him if he had read the James-Wells correspondence.[5] He had and to my surprise seemed rather on Wells's side. "Now if somebody had done a brilliant parody of me like Wells did of James in *Boon*[6] and further had the cheek to send me the book, I'd have answered in kind. James and Wells, unlike Shaw, let every little thing get under their skins. Too bad because Shaw's skin should have been got under—he was so infernally competitive and sure of his superiority. Wells was the only one who did get under his skin. You know, I heard that when Wells died a reporter approached Shaw for a statement. Shaw was waspish, as usual. 'I'm going to die soon, too, you know,' he is supposed to have said."

It was when pursuing a dialectic, however familiar such a one as this must have been, that his voice rose several notches higher than usual. At such times, volubility, not his style in the years I knew him, would pick up. Now he spit out the names in his cast, giving a percussive beat to *Wells, Shaw, James.*

I was fast learning that of all his literary heroes whose work bridged nineteenth and twentieth centuries, Henry James was his favorite, at least at this juncture in his life. At our first meeting, he had allowed me to talk about Maugham and Walpole so *he* could talk about James. Now he was tolerating Wells because it could lead again to James. I was beginning to believe that, for the aging Wilson, James's full-time dedication to literature, his being at most a guest of life when not at his desk, comprised a paradigm.

When Wilson warmed—truly warmed—to a subject, colloquy became monologue. You found yourself carried along.

"James's fiction output actually exceeded Wells's. No other Edwardian was close. I see a good deal, when I'm at Wellfleet, of my friend Leon Edel. He has unearthed some perfectly astounding things which will be in the fourth volume of the biography and about which I am pledged to silence. I knew William James's son Billy at Cambridge. He told me some cruel things about how his father would bait Henry. William would go over to London to visit Henry, who was all anticipation to know the impressions of this American intellectual, his brother. What was the impact of the older civilization on this visitor from the pilgrim shores of Massachusetts? So, according to Billy James, Henry would ask, 'Well, Will, how did you feel when you arrived in London?' and William would say something like 'I felt like I wouldn't be here if I didn't have you to visit.'"

As if feeling guilty about having left our primary topic out to pasture, Wilson got back on track. "James was absurd in his comments on Wells's novel *Marriage.* You remember the dispute. Wells had the principal couple meeting after a cycling accident. They enter a forest and come out an hour or so later openly declaring love for each other. James wrote Wells that this simply wouldn't do. *Marriage* was a failure; it had left out all sorts of psychic material. Strangers simply don't profess love. It couldn't happen that quickly. Well, it could and *does*. Read my story, 'The Princess with the Golden Hair.' It's the largest segment of *Hecate County*, a novel which you should read. I've always felt that book rather underrated by the critics.[7]

"Have you read Max Beerbohm's short parody of James?" he asked. "I must read it to you both. Max is out in two records, you know. Unfortunately, both are at Wellfleet."

We drove to the Towpath at 6:30. Wilson told us it was his favorite among restaurants that were close to home. Mignonne was tending bar; there was no sign of Klaus or their daughter, Monique. She received us standing at attention in the way Wilson liked. We sat in the lounge to await a table. Wilson ordered a double vodka Collins, Jo and I, martinis. He repeated the order before we were seated. He dined on chicken livers and bacon; we, on tenderloin tips in burgundy sauce. He ordered a bottle of dry red Italian wine.

The subject was still Wells, the need for a major biography. I asked him if he had any idea how Gordon Ray, whose authorized biography was announced as in progress as far back as the mid-1950s, was coming along. "I don't know, but I can imagine. Too many people still living who were involved with him. Especially Rebecca West who I think has become a bit dotty. She told somebody that she is the only suffragette who had the courage of her convictions. After all, she did have a son by Wells without being married to him. She was only a little older than Ann Veronica in Wells's novel and can certainly be said to have lived that characterization."

I said I intended to mention Anthony West in my book.

"It may mean, then, that your book can never be published in England. I believe I mentioned before that she's got that restraining order firmly established over there. But you *should* mention the liaison. It was important to both of them. She never quite got over Wells, it would seem."

I asked him if he had ever known any young women who had followed some such fictional example as Ann Veronica.

"It was more a phenomenon in England and on the Continent than here—in a direct line from Ibsen's Nora and Shaw's

Vivie Warren. But Wells's women lovers are rarely developed characters. Even Ann Veronica must strike you as tame today. A writer like Anaïs Nin, a woman who for years has been dramatizing a new feminine point of view, is likely to be influential in ways Wells could never be. I have always thought Anaïs Nin ought to have a large public instead of the special cult that has taken her over."

When we got back to the house, Wilson opened a pint of scotch for hinself and Jo. I had bourbon. He seated us at a long work-table and announced that he was going to read from Max Beerbohm's *A Variety of Things*. He had previewed his choice before we went to the Towpath—"The Guerdon." He explained that Max wrote it in 1916 on the occasion of a posthumous Award of Merit by Edward of England. As a "read" piece, the sketch is irresistible, he said. Written in a style that echoes Jamesian syntax, it portrays the King's predicament at having to honor a name and a man he had never heard of. He tries to sneak a look at a Who's Who without his Lord Chamberlain knowing. "You—you—you see," Wilson translated, the drinks taking their usual vocal toll on him, "it's told from the angle of the Lord Chamberlain who damned well knows the King's dilemma and turns his back obligingly." The parody does not respond well to oral presentation. It would have been difficult for John Gielgud. For Wilson, under the reign of scotch, it proved impossible. When he concluded, I believe it was a relief to all three of us: ". . . in a land that had been under two Jameses and no less than eight Henrys. . . ."

"So you see," Wilson concluded, "Max provides no other clue to the name that was almost deleted than the Henrys and the Jameses." He handed me the book. "I want you to have it."

At the door, he dropped a hint about matters that would color his conversations for the next few years. Going to Switzerland, even though he would be placing Helen in a private school there, would be "like *taking it on the lam*." His voice went up on the colloquialism. "You see, I'm bringing out a tiny book, a pamphlet, really. It's all about the income tax business and the outrageous things the federal government is doing. My Wellfleet neighbor Arthur Schlesinger thinks it's my book that's outrageous. But lay people simply don't read the fine print in the *New York Times*. I've spent the whole summer going over federal tax statutes, mountains of clippings. I'm sure my going abroad will look as if I'm trying to avoid the repercussions."

There was to be an extended stay in London, having to do with the updating of *The Dead Sea Scrolls*. "I've had a terrible time with European Catholics over this. It's all much too complicated to talk about." Yet he had spoken of making his permanent residence in Switzerland. Was our sendoff a final goodbye? He kissed Jo. His last words were to wish me luck with "your Wells book" and to say that mail would be forwarded, wherever he was, if addressed to the Talcottville RD number.

III

"Mr. Wilson, Were You Ever a Communist?"

I myself became irked finally even by the kind of work I was doing writing up strikes and political meetings—from the moment I had definitely the feeling I was working without political direction. . . . But now I don't see any political movement with which I'm prepared to ally myself.—Edmund Wilson, letter to John Dos Passos (May 9, 1935)

I had no premonition that the Soviet Union was to become one of the most hideous tyrannies that the world had ever known.—Edmund Wilson, new Introduction, *To The Finland Station* (1971)

*I*F 1963 had brought three promising encounters with Edmund Wilson, the next year brought an inevitable letdown. He remained "Mr. Wilson," to me and I was "Costa" to him. I should not be surprised if, when the definitive biography is written, it will show that everywhere he went on that sixty-ninth year of his life—in Europe, in Wellfleet, and Talcottville—he remained resolutely out of sorts.

He returned from Europe in May after seven months abroad. He had not settled in Switzerland, and he had not settled his income tax problems. Judging from his *Europe Without Baedeker* dispatches,[1] only the month in Hungary had been satisfactory, "the most interesting country I visited." He complained of bad air and little sunlight in *la ville lumière*. It was a relief, he wrote, finally to be joined by his daughters, Helen from her school in Geneva, Rosalind from Boston, but, he complained, "Rome and Paris are getting more and more like everywhere else—that is, more like the U.S."

We knew from other Upstate members of the benevolent order of Wilsonians that he had made his annual pilgrimage, but our phone did not ring for most of the summer. It came as a surprise, then, at the beginning of August, to hear again the voice whose barely controlled crankiness we knew should not be taken personally. "Heh-heh-hello, Costa? This is Edmund Wilson. I'm just back from Canada. Could you and Mrs. Costa come to dinner Sunday at six? The Towpath. Don't bother to get out of the car. I'll be waiting." As usual, no goodbye. Not even an opportunity to refuse had we wanted to.

Something within the flawed newspaperman was rebelling against the continued cross-examinations of the opportunist academic. Wasn't I *using* the man whose laundry tickets Alfred Kazin once said he would eagerly read if he knew they belonged to Edmund Wilson? Wasn't I thinking mainly of how I might add distinction to an otherwise undistinguished book on H. G. Wells with quotes obtained in person from Wilson? And, after all, would he let me quote him? I would find out Sunday when I determined to check out my book's citations to him.

That night I scoured my typescript for mentions of Wilson. I was surprised at my restraint. If one did not count *acknowledgments*, where I referred to my good fortune as an "accident of geography," I had cited him only twice.[2]

His Towpath claque was waiting for him. A ripple of applause greeted our entrance. Mignonne Heuser congratulated him on the Edward MacDowell Medal that she said had been announced in the *New York Times* that day. I had not seen it. Wilson never pretended modesty. His eyes fastened on Mignonne in the way he had of offering chastisement while not concealing gratitude.

"One tries to ignore these things and ends up taking them seriously," he said. "If enough of them came along, one wouldn't have to work at all." He gave the last phrase that peculiar stress that carried with it, as so many of his remarks did in those days, the implications of his tax troubles. Then he announced that he had just accepted a lucrative residency at the Center for Advanced Studies, Wesleyan University, Middletown, Connecticut. "But I won't have to teach or lecture, merely be there."

He began talking as if his acceptance of the lectureship ("all gravy") was his revenge on those people who "left in droves" when he read at Harvard "from the Civil War book" before publication. "I shall *never* again lecture," he declared. "I might be prevailed upon to *read*. I require full notes, and even then, it's usually disastrous." His voice was biting out the words, a sure sign he was enjoying this, a description of his life-long problem with audiences. "My daughter Rosalind advises me, when speaking publicly, to look at someone—anyone—rather than addressing myself to the back wall. I tried but found it distracting. If it's someone I know, I want to laugh; if someone I don't know, it's embarrassing."

He reserved for another Wilson—Angus—his accolade as the best speaker he had heard recently. "That fellow from Harvard with the three names—you know—oh, yes—*Howard Mumford Jones*—does all sorts of things when he's speaking on a stage—recites Vachel Lindsay—but never has much to say when I see him at the Algonquin."

Reference to the famous hotel reminded him of the time, not long ago, when he was dining there with his friends Mike Nichols and Elaine May. Professor Mark Schorer, who had been May's teacher at Berkeley, walked by. There were introductions. Schorer kept hanging back, seemingly reluctant to leave Wilson's table. Finally, he came out with it. Had Wilson read his new biography of Sinclair Lewis? "I told Schorer that as a matter of fact I had, and I thought it much too long. Schorer kept mumbling something about wondering why Sinclair Lewis thought he was somebody when he wasn't. I suspect Schorer wondered that because he thinks *he's* somebody and isn't."

Now I was warming to the occasion. I have always been convinced that an essay of Schorer's ("Technique As Discovery"[3]), strongly critical of Wells, had a good deal to do with keeping his novels—the good ones like *Tono-Bungay, Kipps*, and *Mr. Polly*—off student reading lists. Ironically, the vogue of science fiction was bringing Wells back into academic favor—and not only the scientific romances.

"But you shouldn't take on Schorer or anybody else in your book," Wilson said emphatically. "I never do. I just write what I believe and cite no one *unless* it's an original view that I adopt too. Van Wyck Brooks taught me that. He never cited anyone unless they were in agreement."

Drinking dominated dining, as usual. Wilson ordered a daiquiri—he pronounced it *dy-kwy-ree*—and kept refills coming. Jo and I stayed with scotch.

On the way back to the house Wilson said, "There's someone I want you two to meet, Malcolm Sharp. He's a lawyer, teaches at the University of Chicago, the husband of a cousin of mine. Dorothy Sharp has been ailing, but I know Malcolm would like to join us." He had me stop the car in front of a small gray house just down the main road from his. "Just sound your horn, he'll come out." While we waited, Wilson went on about Malcolm Sharp. "An interesting combination. Supports the status quo and big business, generally, but is a strong civil-rights man, too. He won't talk about it, but he's written a very good book on the Rosenbergs. After studying the whole record, he concluded they were unjustly tried and unjustly sentenced."

Malcolm Sharp joined us. He could have been Wilson's age, but a full head of hair made him appear fifteen years younger. I sensed he and Wilson would be natural antagonists: the conservative, given to a certain indirectness that may have come from a close study of law; the occasional radical, openly partisan. Once we moved to Wilson's sitting-room and occupied the old-fashioned rockers that filled the room, the two men immediately set up a colloquy, one I found myself not enjoying.

Sharp talked knowledgeably about cases then in the courts. "Jimmy Hoffa will beat the jury-tampering conviction, as he should, but probably go to jail for the union-fund business," he said dispassionately. As it turned out, they were warming up for larger game. The assassination of President Kennedy had occurred while Wilson was in Europe. To listen to Wilson, you would think he had been in Dallas that November, less than nine months ago. The assassination was part of a conspiracy. Ruby had been hired to kill Oswald. The whole case was being put under wraps. Wilson pontificated on these matters as if he had privileged information. Sharp, in his ambiguous way, appeared to agree in large part. Wilson presented in place of evidence his conviction that the Europeans he had talked to at the time of the murder knew more than any of the Americans he had consulted since.

They disagreed over Chief Justice Earl Warren, whom Wilson did not think much of, but of whom Sharp said, "He's a very great man." They agreed that the Warren Commission would get nowhere in its investigation. Wilson thought it fitting that the crime should have been committed in Dallas, and said, not in jest, that he wanted a law that would make it impossible for a Texan to be President. Despite Sharp's efforts to moderate the discussion, the Edmund Wilson we heard that night was talking right out of his curious introduction to his monumental *Patriotic Gore* which shows similarities among Lincoln, Bismarck, and Lenin; gives a short history of United States' imperialism; and likens the U.S. and Soviet Russia to voracious sea slugs preying among smaller organisms.

I was not often to hear Wilson in this frantic vein, especially after he settled up with the IRS two years later.

Finally, Sharp having departed, I summoned up enough courage to show Wilson the citations. He quickly OK'd one about F. Scott Fitzgerald as long as I changed a phrase which might have been taken to indicate his contempt for Wells. "At the time I lent Scott my Wells books, I admired them," he said. Wilson chastened me severely about "minutiae." I had included too much detail on the circumstances of our meetings. I told him I had done this to dispel any suspicion that I was name-dropping. To my delight, he began reading the typescript of a chapter I had titled "The Fall from Grace." When he finished, he looked at me. I shall never forget his words. "It's all very true what you say here." It was one of two precious instances of direct praise for my writing.

At the door he revealed his immediate plans. He would go to the MacDowell Colony for the award on Sunday, the 16th. He expected to remain in Talcottville well into September. We hoped he could have dinner with us. He emphasized that he retired early those days. "I'm still tired from the European habit of late dinners—especially the Italians. They ask you to dinner at six but don't stop drinking until after nine." Jo remarked that his color was fine. Always flattered by someone's concern for his health, he replied that the ravages of the gout do not show on the complexion.

It came as a surprise, then, when our paths crossed in the middle of October. One day early in the semester, Utica College English Chairman Thomas F. O'Donnell called me into his office. Did I know that "a protégée of Wilson's," middle-thirtyish, mar-

ried Hungarian-American woman named Mary Horbach Pcolar
was enrolling in our Continuing Education Program as an English
major? Tom was necessarily vague about her relationship with Wilson. What was clear was that he would be helping to pay her
tuition. Tom said he had just had a chat with the woman and found
her "quite beautiful."

Wilson had suggested that Mary begin her studies in
courses with Tom, our seventeenth-century man, and with me.
She registered for the first term of English literature survey, Chau-
cer to Pope, with Tom, and an elective, Principles of Journalism,
with me.

It was because of Mary's presence in the class that something I should never have suggested actually came about. Wilson
agreed to appear. She made all the arrangements. Continuing
Education classes met one night a week, 6:30 to 9:45, a marathon
agony for most of us. In keeping with Wilson's instructions, relayed
through Mary, there was to be no mention of his coming; he was
not to be required to make any formal presentation; he would
answer questions. After pledging them to secrecy, I invited only
O'Donnell and a close friend from another department, Abe Judson, psychology. Abe, more than anyone I have ever known, was
the embodiment of the loosely applied term "humanist." He was as
well read in American literature as any of the English professors at
Utica College; and he was the living refutation, if any was needed,
of the generalization that psychologists are neurotic. Abe's favorite
novelist was F. Scott Fitzgerald. He had published a monograph
on him, and he was perfectly aware of Wilson's close ties.

I drove to class that night with special tensions added to the
trepidation I always felt at the prospect of filling the 210-minute
period. I had assigned no student panels—the course's ballast—
and was aware that if Edmund Wilson did not appear I would have
to lecture the whole time. In accordance with the injunction, I had
not even told the students about the promised guest. Except, that
is, for two. I assigned one member, a reporter for the college
weekly newspaper, to take close notes and another, F. Kurt Rolfes,
a talented photographer who later became a battle cameraman in
Vietnam, to snap pictures. When I warned him that Edmund Wilson was seventy and unlikely to appreciate bulbs flashing, Kurt
said, "He won't even know I'm taking pictures." And he didn't.

Someone must have leaked the word on Wilson because all twenty-two of the students, Mary excepted, were in their seats at 6:30 when I arrived. I wrote our guest's name on the blackboard and made an announcement that I tried to make sound casual. Now would somebody get up and tell the class about Edmund Wilson? Sepulchral silence. Was it possible? Across my mind, for some reason, swept a James Thurber story about a flunking jock named Bolenciecieccwcz who was unable to supply the name of a mode of transportation even when the prof and the students supplied sounds of whistles tooting and engines chugging. Finally, after what seemed an eternity, an English major, one of two in the class, Mary being the other, spoke up. Hadn't Edmund Wilson written *The Wound and the Bow?* Another warmed to the occasion but confused him with *Colin* Wilson, whose first book, *The Outsider*, was still a campus bestseller.

I asked for a showing of hands. Honest Injun. Seven of the twenty-two had heard of Wilson. I began to talk about him. I was now, for the first time, aware of my two colleagues. I could hear my own voice, a sure sign for me that I am making a hash. Wilson was a literary critic, maybe the best we had. He was a literary man, a man of letters, who did not consider *journalist* a bad word. In fact I quoted him as preferring that designation to *critic*.

My memory of the next ten minutes is vague as to details but vivid as to tone. At one level, I assumed the worst: he simply would not show up. (I had not yet learned that Edmund Wilson was always on time; that Mary Pcolar was as good as her word. Without then knowing it, I had commitments as solid as Gibraltar.) I remember giving in to one indulgence after another, all in the interests of "fill." My eyes kept darting from the lectern to the back of the room. The rooms had glass panels above their doors, the only access to a view outside once the doors were shut. Coat racks extended the length of the corridor. Suddenly, over the door, my roving eye took in a battered hat ascending, suspended on a walking-stick, to the rack; then the stick itself, made by some invisible hand to lie flat; a raincoat came last. All very deliberately. The door opened just as slowly, just a crack. "Are we late, Mary?" Mary, dressed in one of the suits she invariably wore to class, entered behind Wilson. That night he dressed up for the occasion—a charcoal-blue business suit, white shirt with button-down collar, diagonally striped tie.

My most vivid recollection that night was of ungrasped opportunities. Wilson made some sort of brief preamble whose content I have forgotten. There was nothing from him even faintly resembling a patronizing remark about journalism. Rather, he said of contemporary journalists something Somerset Maugham had applied to contemporary novelists. "They are more polished as writers than we were in the twenties and thirties." He went on: "Today there is much more going out on assignment and taking whatever time one needs to get it up. I'm rather spoiled, you know, working for *The New Yorker*. I no longer even receive assignments. No deadlines. I haven't for a long time had to write up anything I wasn't interested in."

There was a single dramatic moment—one dramatic more in retrospect than it was that night. In fact, it passed largely unfelt by the class and even by the academics, including me, who were present. After all, this was 1964, Joe McCarthy was discredited and dead, communism was not so loaded a word. I no longer recall how the subject of Wilson's politics came up. I do recollect that he mentioned Sacco-Vanzetti and his disagreement with his editor at *The New Republic* over the case.[4] He observed, too, that the Stalinist purges ought not to be confused with the ideals of socialism (this was four to five years before he was to meet the celebrated émigré Svetlana Alliluyeva, Stalin's daughter) and that the McCarthy era was a shameful one (he repeated what he had told Chuck Booth and me; i.e., that the McCarthy hearings of a decade ago were virtually the only TV programming he had ever watched). But Edmund Wilson seemed tired; his responses to the questions about politics seemed tired. Then, without any warning, from the back of the room, where Mary Pcolar was sitting:

"Mr. Wilson, *were you ever a Communist?*"

The answer came without a moment's hesitation. "Mary! . . . You must never . . . *never* ask me a question like that again!"

I wish I could say that I recognized—that anyone in the class recognized—what we heard in that exchange as a crystallization of something that is emerging, already in the few years since his death, as an unresolved conflict in the writer and the man. How does one square the seignorial stance with the Marxist apology?

Edmund Wilson never joined the Communist Party. Temperamentally, as anyone who knew him at all would know, he could never have consented to being a party functionary. Daniel

Aaron declares that Wilson was politically "always his own boss. . . . He remained an unspecified radical independent for the rest of his life," Aaron goes on. "As the country moved out of the Depression into war, his briefly held revolutionary expectations dwindled; by the mid-thirties he had already lost whatever hope he ever entertained in the possibility or the desirableness of a Communist system."[5]

Still, as a counter view has it, "Wilson spoke and (in his letters) wrote the standard Marxist gobbledygook of the day; took up the conventional radical animosities against his own country; and . . . supported William Z. Foster, in 1932 the Communist Party candidate for President."[6]

The question may come down to this: whether to "hang" artists like Wilson and Dos Passos for radical activities that may have made it easier for Stalin to devastate a world while men of good will looked on, or to acknowledge their youthful idealisms that, in the wake of the Sacco-Vanzetti execution, questioned probingly every facet of our political and social system.

My own insubstantial conclusion is to apply to Wilson what Frank Swinnerton wrote of his old friend H. G. Wells and his chances of surviving one of his own utopian revolutions: "He would either be put to death by the mandarins for being intractable or would clamor for the restoration of our imperfect, greedy, acquisitive, and amusing society, in which a man could breathe without first obtaining a license to do so. . . . His true passion is for liberty."[7]

In the journalism class that night, the moment passed quickly—for all, apparently, but Mary. Her report to Frederick Exley, which makes up a vital segment of his *Pages from a Cold Island,* gives the impression she had forgotten even her own question although remembering it as "traumatic." Was she seeking to protect the memory of her "Mr. Wilson" from any taint that an unanswered question about Communist connections might introduce? That is my belief. Her version, in Exley's words: "The question was no sooner out of her mouth than Wilson's eagle eyes beneath his massive hawklike brows narrowed furiously, and his forehead bobbed angrily in and out at her, the predator signalling imminent attack."[8] For myself, I cannot remember that the moment picked up the general letdown.'

What I *do* recall were a few much-needed moments of levity. Once, to a student's question about what he thought of the then-recent refusal of Sartre to accept the Nobel Prize, Wilson answered, "Well, it is not anything I would have done." That reply, which brought the evening's best laughs, reflected, I believe, his mounting tax problems, his despair over ever becoming solvent.

The evening's most intelligent question came from Abe Judson. What did Wilson think of the writers of the twenties who had promised a renascence in American literature? Wilson brought hand to pate, then lowered it until he covered his eyes. The best question deserved the best answer. "Yes, they promised us a good bit, but most lacked a second act." As I had first noted in his answers to Booth, he preferred, in public, not to name names. It was clear, from his own writings on Fitzgerald and Hemingway, that early deaths and suicides among his own generation's writers had left him permanently shaken. "Their talents had a somewhat narrow range. They did not, like old wine, age well. Often they wrote the same book over and over."[9]

He did not then speak of something I was thinking as he and Mary took their leave just before the 9:30 mark. Wilson had outlived most of the others. He had *endured.* No wonder Faulkner thought it the most beautiful of words. Wilson was approaching seventy, still productive; he had endured and by persistence left no doubt that the threat posed by his beloved Housman in *To an Athlete Dying Young* could never torment him. This was a matter I was never to hear him verbalize. Could Wilson, Hemingway's first major reviewer and Fitzgerald's literary conscience, have done other than cast himself as one obliged by their default to accept a kind of literary senior statesmanship?

IV

Edmund Wilson at Seventy

*E*DMUND WILSON made one of his rare trips to Talcottville before the summer. It was late in March, still ice-box time Up-state, to see his accountant and to make repairs on the house and the stone barn.

His phone call came from the Club. I was to join him for a drink. Edmund's first question surprised me. Did I know that the only store in Utica where he could buy Beluga caviar had gone out of business? He had just had a depressing chat with the owner. To a generation which would soon take for granted huge shopping centers with chain supermarkets where customers hooked onto cashier's lines whose makeup depended on the number of pur-chases, stores like Planter's of Utica already loomed like charming anachronisms. Mr. Herman Kappel, Planter's proprietor, dis-pensed conversation while directing newcomers to the right stall. Leah Kappel, enclosed in a rear office but accessible behind a booth window, moved from rolltop desk and telephone to cashier's station as the occasion demanded. No ordinary neighborhood store, Planter's recently had had to give up its delivery service to places like Clinton ten miles south.

Now Planter's, with its unduplicated stocks of imported rare foods, was no more. Wilson saw the passing of the Utica institution—the unavailability of Beluga caviar for his sand-wiches—as still another sign of cultural ebb. They were Spenglerian omens of the decline of the middle class everywhere. I should be sure to read Ortega y Gasset's *Revolt of the Masses*. I asked him if this wasn't a curious recommendation for the author of *To the Finland Station* to be making. He looked at me curiously—was this, like Mary Pcolar's question to him last fall, one no one was to ask? He chose to ignore the remark. Instead he told me about a grocery in Hyannis, Massachusetts, which, like Planter's, had gone down the drain. Did I see any hope anywhere?

"You're a journalist," he said. "You're in touch. Do you see anyone hopeful emerging in public life?"

I replied that I thought LBJ's Great Society looked like a continuation, even an implementation, of the dead John F. Kennedy's ideals. It was the wrong ploy. "I don't believe he's upholding Kennedy at all," Edmund shot back. "He already believes that writers are people he has got to be against because he thinks they're against him. Is that following in Kennedy's footsteps?"

Edmund's loyalty to the late President was understandable. In 1961 he had been one of the thirty-three recipients of the Presidential Medal of Freedom, the highest civilian honor in the United States. He noted in *Upstate* that when *The Cold War and the Income Tax* was due to be published, just after the award, he sent his friend Arthur Schlesinger the proofs of the pamphlet and asked him to be sure that Kennedy knew what was in it before he presented the medal. Years later Wilson learned from another source that the President was forwarded a sixteen-page memorandum in opposition to making the award to E.W. When Kennedy saw the man who was leading the fight against Wilson, he is reported to have said, "This is not an award for good conduct but for literary merit."[1]

Over drinks at the Fort Schuyler, Edmund seemed out of sorts, unhappy with the year he was spending at the Center for Advanced Studies, a man on the eve of his seventieth birthday. Not even the effects of Johnny Walker at "happy hour" could lift his spirits. I told him that the book I always read when at lowest ebb was *Notes from Underground*. The book, contrary to the effect it is supposed to have, always left me exhilarated.

Wilson demurred. Dostoevsky was a terrible stylist, he said, and since he only read the Russians in the original, he would come out of the experience further depressed. "I've been going back to Maurice Baring," he said. "In his novels, everyone is culti-vated, well bred, cosmopolitan. I try to remember that society, even in America, used to be like that."

I sensed his mood, not so much by the catalog of disasters of the aging that he recited but by the rare failure of cheer to leak through. It was not the heavy snowfalls he minded, even though they delayed the repairs he had come Upstate to oversee. In fact, he found it joyous, waking up that first morning in Talcottville and finding himself, not in the large house set aside for him and his fellow scholars at Wesleyan but in his own house. But, right from the start, paralyzing things began to happen. He was no sooner up, ready to get to his writing, than the phone rang. Mabel Hutchins, whom he depended upon to lay out his meals, had had an opera-tion, a tumor removed from her spine, and was in the hospital in Utica.

This kind of news always tended to lower his spirits. People like Mabel Hutchins were family; he felt responsible for all the Talcottville/Boonville people, especially those of his generation. How could he manage, at the old house in the middle of the long Upstate winter, without Mrs. Hutchins?

And all was not going well with Mary. After earning A's in her courses last fall, she had had what Wilson called "a kind of breakdown." She had been working full-time as the assistant to the manager of a large pharmacy in Rome while carrying demanding upper-level courses in the Romantics and the Victorians, both on the same 3¼-hour, one-night-a-week basis. As anyone knows who tries to cover literary periods in a single semester of only fifteen meetings, the reading assignments are overwhelming. She com-plained to Wilson about being lectured to on Wordsworth and Coleridge without understanding a word and of having to read between meetings *Nostromo* and *Pickwick Papers*.

"I tried to read *Nostromo,* so as to be some help to Mary, but I found it no easier going than when I first opened it while an undergraduate. Friends tell me the book gets off the ground after the first hundred pages, but I break down long before that." Then he broke into a tirade against Conrad generally, even *Lord Jim,* another book he had tried and failed with; a book whose multiple ambiguities of viewpoint were for him *longueurs* of a writer who could not make anything happen.

"How about *Pickwick?*" I asked.

"I adored Dickens at college and reread everything for my 'Two Scrooges'² essay, but I am beyond taking on *Pickwick* at this late date, even for Mary."

He said that he was reading the Victorian novelists he had missed—George Eliot, especially. "I'm reading *Middlemarch* in the evenings. I can imagine living life in the manner of a George Eliot chronicle. In fact, I am, and I don't especially like it."

Mention of *Middlemarch* led me to a confession, perhaps the first really personal aside I had allowed myself with him. I was planning, at *forty-three*, to go to graduate school, at Purdue, for the doctorate. I related to Edmund that my sense of inferiority among colleagues who were all so much better read than I had become an obsession. I was going back to school to do some reading.

I wish I could write that Edmund gave immediate and enthusiastic endorsement. Instead, with that gesture of his that I had come to associate with a sense of futility—the way he would bring the palm of his right hand hard across his right eye—he simply said, "I think your trouble is that you don't write enough. When is your Wells book coming out anyway?"

I made my second confession. The editor had returned the manuscript for major revisions. I had no idea when the book would be out. Without warning, and for the first time, Edmund began to talk about Wells in the way I had fantasized he might three years ago and more when I wrote him for the first time.

"The influence of H. G. Wells, and of course of Shaw, too, was tremendous on persons of my generation." He brought two fingers to his temple, allowing them to crease the skin. It was a way he had when about to deliver a catechism. You simply waited at such moments. "B-b-but I can remember the exact moment—the scene—after which I stopped reading Wells altogether." He paused again, moving his hand from temple to the fringe of hair behind his ear. "It was in a novel of his called *The Research Magnificent*. You've read it, of course? The Wells scientist—can't remember his name any longer—stands alone in the jungle facing a Bengal tiger. Wells has this fellow, unarmed, raise his hand before this fiercest of the cats. 'I am man,' he says. The tiger just walks away. After that bit of nonsense, I haven't been able to read a line of Wells, except his earliest things, in forty years!"

He continued non-stop, his voice rising when it came time

for a put-down, levelling off, seemingly, to call back a still bright memory of the first Wells, the exhilarating, anything-is-possible Wells. Was I hearing an echo of a younger Wilson that I knew only from things I had read? Was this someone like the Miles Murphy of Mary McCarthy's *roman à clef* who "tends to lecture rather than converse . . . all through dinner"?[3] Was I seeing in action the Wilson whose "reality" brought "terror" to at least one female peer who spurned his marriage proposal?[4]

The lecture promised to go on indefinitely. "I have come to believe that the influence of Wells and Shaw on my generation, in the final analysis, may have been damaging. They were too Rousseauvian. Their novels and plays never go on to trace the outcome of the polygamous situations they herald. Many saw in these works carte blanche and were irreparably injured."

Had Edmund Wilson, like his friend John Dos Passos, moved full circle? Did he see the golden influences of his youth, the impetus to passades and Marxism alike, turned metallic as now, in old age, he was turning to pastoral?[5]

Lecture complete, Edmund built himself to his feet, shuffled to the window of the Club. Although the calendar had announced spring, and April only a few days away, snow began flaking down. He announced he would remain overnight. I was relieved. Even a light snow would make Deerfield Hill hazardous. We parted early.

In June, when I saw him again he sounded more chipper. Yes, he would be delighted to come to dinner on the fifteenth. Tom and Gert O'Donnell would join us. Could I pick him up in Talcottville in time to see the Social Security people? As it turned out, Jo called for him, drove him to the Fort Schuyler in the morning, and I picked him up at three. His Club was the one place in Utica where he was at ease—like him, a relic of end-of-century Americana that had survived.

Named for the fortification where Major General Philip J. Schuyler of the Continental Army delayed the three-pronged advance of the British forces on Albany in 1777 and contributed to the defeat of Burgoyne at Saratoga, the Club also bore, for me, a socially strategic location in downtown Utica. The Fort Schuyler is situated on Genesee and Court at what, living from 1948–51 in an apartment on Genesee across the street, I came to consider the city's melting-pot. On weekend nights, before the days of TV, all of Utica seemed to converge on the Stanley Theater (Warner Brothers), a door or two from the apartment building I occupied and catty-cornered from the Club. I would observe—"going to the show"—the Italians from the East end, the Poles and Germans from West Utica, the Welsh from Corn Hill a few blocks toward the then-luxurious Parkway on the Southeast, and the by-then minority Wasps from South Utica and suburban New Hartford.

The Fort Schuyler Club may have been Utica's last social institution to give up its "privacy." Entrance is still by membership only. However, until after World War II, all but the original Utica families were kept out. These were the founders of the knitting mills. In the early 1950s, about the time when the textile factories either dissolved or moved South, new and younger members were permitted to join. Oridinarily—that is, unless the family was affluent—none of the "minority" people who flocked to the Stanley were invited. Wilson begins mentioning "the Schuyler" in his letters of the early sixties. By that time, increasing expenses were causing a more "open" membership. Wilson observes in *Upstate* that elderly men always predominated.

I could see one of the elderly men through the front window, his nose buried in a magazine. I waved and Edmund waved back. I followed as he shuffled to the coat rack where he found the crumpled tan raincoat ("mine's the one with the tear in it"), the floppy hat, the walking-stick. He looked feebler than I had ever seen him. He handed me the address of the Social Security office. It was only two blocks away, but he preferred to drive, and I soon learned why. He had had a mild heart attack three nights ago at the old house. "I've had a heart condition, you know—had it for years but no trouble for some time. Dr. Smith,[6] our Boonville G.P., startled me by dropping back this morning for tests. He tells me I'll be fine but no climbing and as little walking as possible."

I let him off at the Social Security office and returned forty-five minutes later. I saw an elderly man, the familiar hat on the desk beside him, in animated conversation with an attractive female counselor. I wondered if it would mean anything, even to one of them, to know that the little man with the high color and aristocratic nose—the old man inquiring about Social Security coverage upon reaching seventy—was America's foremost man of letters. Edmund was enormously impressed by the fact that S.S. was about to become fully programmed by computers. "They tell me that a computer has registered my eligibility and that my check, to the exact amount, will be made out automatically and dispatched to me."

I had to wait about a half-hour. I kept noticing the darting in and out of the manager of the office, a man with whom I was acquainted from my years as a newspaperman. Clearly he was waiting for the famous man to finish his business. The manager could not avoid walking by me; I smiled; he returned mine with a perfunctory one of his own. After about three such brushes, he would look at me quickly, then not at all. When, finally, Edmund shuffled toward the door, the manager greeted him with elaborate apologies for not having been in his office to receive Wilson personally. Then, upon seeing that Edmund was with me, the manager became deferential to an extreme, this time apologizing for not having greeted *me* before. Edmund was amused when I told him about the manager's quick-change artistry.

We arrived at my house shortly after five. It was now "Jo," "Edmund," and "Dick," although we occasionally lapsed into "Mr. Wilson." In all the time we were to know him, we never heard anyone refer to him as "Bunny," the nickname his mother gave him and a burden to him, among Princeton friends and earlier ones, all his life. Clearly "Bunny" was among the ghosts he left behind at Wellfleet.

Was it something Italianate that he saw in Jo (a kind of Papal Connection?) that induced Edmund to launch a mock serious tirade against the Roman church? Perhaps what did it was my asking him how he was enjoying the year at Wesleyan. His favorite, he said, among all the scholars at the Center for Advanced Studies was Father Cyril D'Arcy, who he said had presided at the conversions of Evelyn Waugh and Graham Greene. He told an elaborate story about the Vatican and the Communists which he said was related to him by Ignazio Silone during a sojourn to Rome in 1945. Some anti-Papal articles were appearing in the Italian press. It was clear to the clergy that they were being written by someone on the inside. Investigation unearthed evidence that the journalist had been a Vatican writer who, assigned to make a study of Marxism, had become so enraptured that he renounced his Catholicism and went over to the Communists. Later, according to Silone's story, Wilson version, the fellow was written off by the Reds who had recently taken the "ecumenical business" to heart and felt better relations with the Vatican were mandatory. They banished him to Albania.

Edmund was interested to learn that I had once met Jerre Mangione, a writer of his acquaintance, too, and one who was in Sicily at that time doing a book on Danilo Dolci. Wilson had met Dolci, the Gandhi of Sicily, and found him uncommunicative. "I felt there was an analogy between our treatment of the American Indian and the lot of the Sicilians," he said. "Dolci showed no interest in anything I said. For good reason, perhaps. This was in May of 1945, just after V-E Day. There had been wild excitement during the first days of the expulsion of the Germans, the Mussolini execution, and so forth, but immediately afterwards everybody relapsed into a kind of state of tense exhaustion. At the end of the evening after I'd had the disappointing meeting with Dolci, his people passed a hat around. Silone now doubts Dolci's ability to accomplish anything in Sicily but at least regards him higher morally than he does André Malraux, whom he—unfairly, I believe—thinks of as a 'nihilist'—someone who wants to get results without caring about the moral purpose of what he does."

I reminded Edmund that Silone kept rewriting his old books, *Pane, Vino* and, most recently, *Fontamara*. He picked up on this eagerly. "Most of us are sick to death of our books even before they're published, but Silone always rewrites his to accord with his latest views. He's a remarkable man but a little too spiritual for me. He is a queer mixture of priest and Communist underground worker. Women, I believe, are taken by the priest in him. His wife Darina told me she fell in love with his books before she married him and has been rereading them since. She's Irish, you know, and given to taking periodic vacations from marriage, all apparently with his blessing. She's still a beautiful woman, and I don't wonder that she finds Silone not always ah-ah-adequate. Perhaps the spiritual side comes up at the wrong times." Wilson chuckled, then paused. He would often do that only after some such formulation as the one on Silone. It was as if he wanted to register it, file it away, without having to excuse himself to make a note.

The O'Donnells arrived—Tom and Gert. Wilson exploited their coming to extend his stories of adventures with Roman Catholicism. (I kept hoping at points like this that he would mention Mary McCarthy, but he was not to do so until one of our last conversations, and then in a single word.) Without a hint of patronization, Edmund observed that all the interesting people at the Center were Catholics—from the director, the novelist Paul Horgan, on down. "The most stimulating scholar this year is Father D'Arcy, against whom I had rather a prejudice, I admit." He related to the O'Donnells what he had told us.

O'Donnell, never one to back off, entered into an animated discussion about the controversy between the Dominicans and the Jesuits. Edmund said he had admired the liberality of the Jesuits until a reviewer on the staff of the Jesuit magazine *America* sent him the original proofs of a review of *The Dead Sea Scrolls*. Wilson understood why when he read the published review, an essay that had been severely cut and changed from favorable to unfavorable.

The year at Wesleyan had not been a happy one. Tom had asked him about it, perhaps expecting the opposite response. Tom, a loyal Hamilton man, considered Wesleyan one of the few smaller liberal arts colleges that merit being mentioned in the same breath. Edmund complained that Middletown offered nothing and that, except for a nucleus of good students ("the ones who went to Selma, demonstrate, and all that sort of thing"), the level is not high. Tom noted that Wesleyan's library was reputedly one of the best undergraduate collections in the United States. "I don't know anything about that," said Edmund. "I never visited it. We could send out couriers for anything we wanted."

He continued to speak affectionately about Paul Horgan. When he mentioned his new glasses, of a rimless kind recommended by Horgan, I knew what I'd found changed in him when we met that afternoon. A disquisition on eye glasses followed. He had had his father's gold-rimmed spectacles fitted with his own prescriptions. "They're my Ben Franklins," Edmund cracked.

Edmund downed four martinis quickly; his spirits were

high from the start. When Jo called us to dinner, we moved to the diningroom which overlooked our Sauquoit Valley. The scene moved regionalists Wilson and O'Donnell to exchange affectionate tributes to Upstate. Tom, a native, could never be happy anywhere else. Al the finest prose stylist on the faculty, he lavished much of that style on his beloved region. Edmund agreed. "We live in what is unquestionably one of the most beautiful places on earth."

Edmund led the conversation through dinner and after. He always went to great lengths to avoid repeating a story. He might have already launched one before pulling up short: "But you must be sure to tell me if you've heard any story I tell." He was not as insincere in this connection as most professional raconteurs; he would not have minded, at least in his old age, at being stopped in mid-story. I never heard anyone stop him, and I don't recall him ever repeating a story.

It had been arranged that I would drive Edmund to Talcottville before eight, but Tom, breaking in a new Oldsmobile, asked if he might drive up Deerfield Hill in order to pad the gauge for the 1,000-mile checkup. I deferred gladly. So, leaving Jo and Gert, we piled in, Wilson in the front.

I knew Tom was anxious to discuss the Utica-born novelist Harold Frederic (1856–98), about whom he had co-authored a book. Edmund, in the midst of a spiritual quest to learn everything he could about the region where his relatives had settled, was planning a piece on Frederic for *The New Yorker*. Tom, not one to hold back with something on his mind, may have deferred to me, non-regionalist that I am. He did not bring up his favorite topic. So I did. We stopped momentarily at Tom's Utica College office. He returned to the car with a boxful of manuscripts: Frederic stories and memorabilia, a little-known first edition.

Edmund in his usual pattern was then working on a number of projects simultaneously. Much of his research revolved about his ancestors, the settlers of Lewis County, the Talcotts, the literature of the region. The two talked about John W. De Forest. Tom observed that it was William Dean Howells who urged Frederic to write of the region he (Frederic) knew so well, and it was also Howells who, to Frederic's everlasting disappointment, never acknowledged a worshipfully inscribed copy of Frederic's best novel, *The Damnation of Theron Ware*.

Tom talked fluently of these things. Wilson remained silent a long time. Then, as if he were in the classroom and wanted a particular student to speak up, Tom put a direct question. "Mr. Wilson, do you think *Damnation* is a great novel?" It was the kind of question he usually parried if he thought his opinion was no better than the next person's. But Harold Frederic *mattered*. I shall never forget Edmund's answer. "It's an important novel, historically and otherwise, but it is not a great one. It is not great because no great work has ever been built on the humiliation of its hero."

A fascinating point but one that caught Tom and me by surprise. I did not then know *Damnation* well enough to counter. However, the silence of O'Donnell, who has read every line Frederic wrote, was surprising. One had a sense, after Edmund's pronouncement, that the case for *Damnation* was closed.[7]

Our drive to Talcottville was by twilight, an appropriate coloring for me because it consisted of an unsuccessful series of attempts to deflect Wilson from his regional *persona*. I had seen with some surprise that the current *PMLA Bibliography* had listed an article Wilson had written on Max Beerbohm. I asked him about it. He said he had submitted the piece to *Encounter*[8] rather than to *The New Yorker* "because Sam Behrman is working on his own Beerbohm memoir." Max is better than modern cartoonists, Edmund believed, because he never did a caricature of anyone he had not met or talked with. He was displeased by the "owlish job" that had just been done of him by a caricaturist for *The New York Review of Books*.

I asked Edmund, for both our benefits, Tom's and mine, what he thought of the various books in the Twayne Authors series. "Often they are very bad. I've just read the George Ade—just awful. The series are nonselective. So many names barely known at all." *The New Yorker* sent them all to him ("to get rid of them"), but he rarely read any of them unless one had some pertinence to the writing he was then doing. The O'Donnell-Franchere book on Harold Frederic struck him as an exception—"one of the good ones, enormously informative and helpful." He expressed surprise that Tom had contracted with Twayne for a second book, this one on James Kirke Paulding.[9] Wilson thought little, and knew less, of Paulding. He asked Tom if he had read the recent Twayne on

Edward Arlington Robinson. They agreed Robinson was a great poet, "especially in the short things," Wilson said, and under-rated, particularly in comparison to Frost (". . . so much better," Wilson thought, "than Frost who, as we now know hated every-body and was something of an old fraud").

The bringing to light of the other—the unsavory—Robert Frost suggested to Wilson the difficulty of publishing memoirs and other autobiographical material while one was alive. "One of my notebooks is almost ready—no one living will be hurt—but there's so much more that can't come out now."[10] (Wilson always spoke about the writings of his that had to await his death dispassionately, as cultural history. I have always thought that their existence was a constant reminder to him that death might be near.)

Occasionally, in the midst of one of his genealogical excur-sions or Tom's regional notations, my ears would perk up. Edmund had come on something like a scoop. "Did you know that Wynd-ham Lewis had Upstate origins? He had told me he was born in Philadelphia; somebody else had it that he was born on a boat in the mid-Atlantic; while he was working in Toronto, he claimed Canada. I'd got the feeling he was illegitimate. The fact is, though he never admitted it, that he was born not far from Schenectady, in Livingston County."[11] Mention of Lewis and his obscure link to Central New York reminded Tom of an Ezra Pound story. Just before World War II, Pound returned to his alma mater Hamilton College to receive an honorary degree. Pound sat on the stage during commencement and bronx-cheered H. V. Kaltenborn, the main speaker, whose political views on Fascist Italy did not coin-cide with Pound's. The conclusion of Tom's story seemed to be a signal for one of Edmund's—a rare bombshell. "Pound's son Omar was actually sired by William Butler Yeats, you know." We did *not* know and still don't.[12] Tom and I looked at each other, neither wishing to show ignorance.

Edmund insisted that we stop at his place for a nightcap. He bade us stop at the liquor store in Boonville to pick up a bottle of Johnny Walker Red. As it turned out, he finished the pint single-handed. We both had classes next day. The Jesuitical colloquy resumed. Finally, at the door, Edmund did something I have often observed in drinkers-in-their-cups. They remind the sober to be-ware of someone else's drinking. Edmund warned me, with half-seriousness about Philippe (Phito) Thoby-Marcelin, a Haitian poet and friend of Malcolm Lowry, to whom he was to introduce me later that summer. "Don't let Phito drink as much as he'd like. He becomes unintelligible—in English *and* in French." I could have said Thoby-Marcelin was not the only one. "By the way, Elena will be coming up here with our daughter for the Fourth of July; then we'll all drive back to Wellfleet." His children by other marriages, Rosalind and Reuel, and Elena's people were all converging on Wellfleet, it appeared, and that would cut short his summer Upstate.

Tom and I drove back to Utica, our talk filled with Wilson. I had known him now for three years, Tom for a year or so less. To me, before we met, he was the popularizer of *Finnegans Wake,* whose "translation" I had read twenty years ago without much comprehension, in *The New Yorker*.[13] I recall, when I first mentioned to Tom the possibility of meeting our famous literary neighbor to the north, he had referred to Edmund Wilson as "crotchety."

Now he was our friend. Time enough for both of us to have been wrong.

V

From a Distance

I DID NOT SEE EDMUND for more than a year after the encounters in the spring and summer of 1965. In fact, I saw little even of my family during the 1965–66 academic year. We agreed, Jo and I, that the only way we could manage the first year in graduate school would be for me to take the research fellowship offered at Purdue while she taught that year at the small centralized high school in Sauquoit. Within weeks of starting doctoral studies, I knew I could not hope to finish the course work in less than two years and two summers. If all went well, Jo and Philip, who had just turned ten, would join me in Indiana for the second year of my residency.

I continued to correspond with Edmund Wilson during that first year. He loomed in multiple roles. Surely it was not simply kindness, or the availability of my car, that had prompted him to allow me entry to his north country seigniory. That recognition, a kind of fortifying by association, buoyed me up for the difficult transition.

Except for one kindred older graduate student who shared office space in Heavilon Hall across from the editorial offices of *Modern Fiction Studies,* I never could bring myself to mention Wilson. Always bemused and often contemptuous of academic overkill in literary scholarship—his war with the Modern Language Association was three years away[1]—Edmund Wilson could not be neatly fitted into any of our critical pigeonholes. As befitted the "public critic" nonpareil, no tag was appropriate. His readers comprised that indefinable category of non-student students, literates who welcomed the "translation" of demanding texts and ideas in them to graspable paraphrase.

A peculiar set of circumstances, extracurricular and curricular, kept Edmund much on my mind that first year. For one thing, I wrote an unsigned newsletter for *Modern Fiction Studies* (founded at Purdue in 1952). These book reviews kept my desk piled with current critical and scholarly texts on twentieth-century fiction. Writing them took the place of teaching freshman composition and grading fifty themes a week.

One of the first books I reviewed at any length involved two of my heroes—Maugham, directly, and Wilson, indirectly. It was *The Two Worlds of Somerset Maugham*, by Wilmon Menard.[2] The book purported to be based on long interviews with Maugham but was actually a piecing together of ideas and quotations that Menard had drawn wholecloth, and without attribution, from W.S.M.'s *The Summing Up*. Menard's expressed aim was to unearth the true stories behind Maugham's tales of the South Seas. Possessing undoubted familiarity with Polynesia, the author filled portions of the book with dime-store anthropology, then used Maugham stories, real and imagined, as connectives. Menard's travels, admittedly, had uncovered some fascinating material. For example, the name "Miss Thompson" appeared on a passenger list of a Sydney-bound steamer *Sonoma*, which in early December 1914 stopped off at Pago Pago, the capital of Eastern Samoa. The list, from a back issue of a Honolulu newspaper, revealed that Maugham, creator of Sadie Thompson, was also on board. But the palpable "steals" from *The Summing Up* made the whole enterprise suspect.[3]

It was the opening of the book, however, that made me wince and write—to Edmund Wilson. It begins with a cocktail party at the Rapallo villa of Max Beerbohm "in the early 1950s." Maugham was there and "sulking," according to Menard, because of the possibility that Wilson would be there too. Here is Beerbohm talking, Menard version:

> "When Willie arrived I made the mistake of mentioning to him that one of your critics, Edmund Wilson, might be here

today, too. Fortunately, Wilson couldn't make it. Anyway, because Willie loathes Wilson for some rather uncomplimentary things he wrote about his talents—and for the possibility that they might have been in the same company—he's thoroughly provoked at me, and is in the library sulking. However, he is alone, and perhaps by now he's simmered down a bit. Let's hope so."

Menard continues in his own words:

I recalled that Edmund Wilson, once notorious for his *Memoirs of Hecate County,* had given Maugham's *Then and Now* a scathing review when it was published in 1946. He had taken the opportunity to make a disparaging summation of all his writings, and had included a most unflattering character-analysis as well.

Wilson had relegated him, with perverse waspishiness, to the category of a second-rate author, accusing him of shoddy craftsmanship, character delineation and plotting; he insinuated that Maugham had venomously used his position as a "popular writer" to attack far superior writers, and had also attempted to promulgate false standards of morality and undermine the precepts of Christianity. Specifically Wilson had said: "It has happened to me from time to time to run into some person of taste who tells me that I ought to take Somerset Maugham seriously. Yet I have never been able to convince myself that he was anything but second-rate. . . ." It would have been better, Wilson sneered, if Maugham had continued with his early medical career and left serious writing to those better equipped. (pp. 30–31)

Maugham's death in his ninety-second year, in 1965, coincided insidiously with the publication of Menard's book. I opened my review by suggesting that Somerset Maugham would have fallen less easily into his final sleep if he had known *The Two Worlds* was due to be published. That so much of it was a shameless adopting to his own purposes of Maugham's already published words made me assume, perhaps unfairly, that Menard's book was all a fraud. So I wrote to Wilson to see if he had any recollection of such an invitation to Beerbohm's villa at Rapallo.

Edmund answered by return mail: "I don't believe that Maugham-Beerbohm story. I was never in Rapallo except that time in '54 that I tell about in *Bit*, & then there was no Somerset Maugham in the offing. . . . In my article on Maugham, I said nothing about his 'abandoning the principles of Christianity'—not being a Christian myself—& nothing to the effect that it would have been better if he had gone on with his medical career. [Menard] misstates my mention of this." A new biography of Maugham further casts Menard's version in doubt. It also quotes Maugham as sympathizing with Wilson in his plight with the Internal Revenue and referring to him as "the most brilliant man you have, you know."

The letter about Maugham also solicited information about a criticism he had made of *Ulysses* in *Axel's Castle*, this question having originated in a seminar on Joyce. Once we had worked our way quickly through the *Portrait* and the stories in *Dubliners*, we settled down to taking up *Ulysses* chapter by chapter. I asked Wilson to reassess his viewpoint, thirty-five years after the publication of *Axel's Castle*, that the extraordinary *monologues intérieurs* of *Ulysses* were compensatory measures by a writer who was unable to *move* his narrative at a faster pace: "Do you still feel that the minutiae that are stockpiled in *Ulysses* are compensations for Joyce's inability to produce pace and movement? I am working on my final paper for the Joyce seminar, a comparison of *Ulysses* and *Under the Volcano*. Do you still feel that way about *Ulysses*?" Edmund's reply, contained in the same letter, was characteristically to the point. "Yes: I am still of that opinion about *Ulysses*—also, about *Finnegans Wake*."

I had not always appreciated the laconic in his style. I resented *The New Yorker's* replacement of Clifton Fadiman's charming weekly essays by Wilson's terse critiques. I remained for years puzzled by Fadiman's admission that he had written thousands of words of reviewing but not a single word of literary criticism.[4] Now, separated from Fadiman's successor by nearly a thousand miles but joined to him, too, by recent memory and the reading of his books, I was beginning to understand the difference.

That lonely first year away from home could not end too soon. I left for Utica as soon as I could finish the current *Modern Fiction Studies* Newsletter which included reviews, largely descriptive, of the two books Edmund had published in 1965. We stayed only a few days before packing off, the three of us, for British Columbia where I was to spend most of the summer at the Malcolm Lowry Special Collection, University of British Columbia. Reinforced for the start of the second year by the presence of Jo and Phil, I found a letter awaiting me at Purdue. It contained thanks for the *MFS* reviews and a final paragraph that was far from shop talk:

> . . . I'll feel a good deal better about you people when I know you are back in Utica.
>
>   Best regards to you and Jo,
>
>   Edmund W.

☙ VI ❧

Solvency and Settlement

IN A REVIEW OF *Edmund Wilson: Letters on Literature and Politics: 1912–1972* Harry Levin notes that Wilson was not free from financial insecurities until his late sixties.[1] This is certainly an accurate dating for anyone who knew him throughout the 1960s. From the time I met him, in 1963 when he was sixty-eight, until I went off to graduate school two years later, the subject of his insolvency always crept into our conversations. There were always two visitations whose primacy I took for granted: the trip to see his dentist in Lowville and the even more doleful journey in the other direction to see his accountant in Utica. The bitterness and acrimony that produced his least responsible book, *The Cold War and the Income Tax* (1964), were laid to rest between his seventieth and seventy-first birthdays (May 1965–May 1966), a period during which he made peace with the IRS, or so his Utica attorney Francisco Penberthy told me in 1974; he was presented a medal and $1,000 by the American Academy of Arts and Sciences and the $5,000 National Medal for Literature. It was only the second of the latter awards, the first recipient having been Thornton Wilder. He was nearing forty when he took on the mercurial life of a free-lance. His self-made assignments, which became well-paid pieces in *The New Yorker* and then books, provided continuous travel; his life, until old age slowed him, was as transient as a foreign correspondent's and as sedentary as that of George Gissing's Henry Ryecroft.

Returning from Vancouver to Utica for the month of August, I obtained a four-week assignment nights on the copydesk of my old paper, and, for the first time ever, I telephoned Wilson. Knowing that his book on Canada was about to appear, we were eager to tell him of our first visit to the Canadian interior. But he was brusque, not at all as I thought he should be with a friend he had not seen for a year. It occurred to me that he might even have turned down our invitation if it had not been for the promised presence of Phito and Eva Thoby-Marcelin. When I picked him up at Talcottville at five o'clock, his appearance dispelled my doubts. He was in stocking feet. He bade me sit down while he set to work putting on his shoes. Elena was supposed to have been there, but she had caught a virus which twice put off her arrival. I asked him if he minded being alone at night in the big house. "No, not at night," he said.

During the forty-five-minute drive to Utica, Edmund talked of the $5,000 award in a way that was unusual for him: flippantly. Tom O'Donnell, who had seen him earlier in the summer, reported Edmund's complaints that his bank accounts were exhausted and he had no immediate income. The $5,000 had saved him. He expressed none of this. Rather, he described the award as a means to lure him to New York to speak at a PEN affair. "I fooled them, pleaded that I didn't feel up to New York. Instead I arranged to be in Utica for the award. That way I escaped all the fuss and got the money, too."

What I was hearing once again, as we drove down Deerfield Hill, was an effect of Edmund's blend of distrust in a literary establishment that lionized him but rarely rewarded him and his native insistence on the craftsman's spartanism that accepted as necessary the sacrifices of the professional. Out of this uneasy truce between his suspicions that the life of letters was being undermined and his ethic that work was all that really counted came all those jockeyings between his two free-lance outlets, *The New Yorker* and *The New York Review of Books*, and the invariable, and prompt, transplant of every word, however ephemeral, from commissioned article to book. His generation, as he had told my class, was not outfitted well for survival, but he was.

As we neared Utica, Edmund spoke of a short play he had written which he said was about to be published simultaneously in both periodicals.[2] "It's a satire of the academic life, all about a professor of Elizabethan literature who has written a play that he pirated from a little-known original. I've had some trouble with *The New Yorker*. I have the professor use *furkin*, a perfectly good Elizabethan word. At one point he says he hopes so-and-so 'will give her a thoroughgoing furkin.' *The New Yorker* made me take out the word, which would be in perfectly good use as either an old unit for ale or of weight, generally; *The New York Review of Books* let it go. Of course I wrote the play to be produced, too."

He spoke with the same air of flippancy he had used to talk about the $5,000 when he discussed the recent sale of his papers to Yale. "Texas made the highest offer, but I didn't care for the man they sent up. I can get over to New Haven more easily than I can travel to Austin, Texas." This mention of university archive purchases enabled me for the first time to talk about the Canadian trip. I told Edmund of meeting Basil Stuart-Stubbs, the University of British Columbia rare-books man. Stubbs was put out at the Texas people who could outbid everyone. They had been willing to pay huge sums for Xeroxed copies of the Malcolm Lowry collection. Stubbs said he refused to send them anything. "When a school already has the reigning collection of a writer, the richer schools ought not to horn in," Wilson declared.

He spoke of his current labor—the working up of his notebooks. He was preparing the World War I and *New Republic* material, dating from 1919. "So much that can't be published until after my death," he muttered as an aside, a refrain I had heard before and would hear again. "Have you read my *Daisy* novel?" he broke in. "You know, it's surprising how it stays in print. An Englishwoman, just over serious illness and fighting back—wrote me that the book gave her courage. I can't imagine what she meant." Roger Straus— Edmund never referred to his publishers as "Farrar, Straus & Giroux"; he always used the name of his friend, the senior member—wanted, he said, to bring out an edition of his works, but there were problems with four other publishers who held copyright to one or more of the works.

Edmund knew that the Thoby-Marcelins were to join our group that evening. The Wilson-arranged meeting with Phito and Eva last summer became something more than a chance for me to talk to one who had known Malcolm Lowry. The four of us struck it off immediately: Phito, an artist of great dignity which never prevented twinkles of humor from breaking in; Eva, handsome, always on the lookout to install a human deflection of any tendency to pomposity. Edmund loved them singly, but especially as a couple; their friendship went back nearly two decades. What Edmund did not know—we had been briefed earlier—was that Phito's younger half-brother, Pierre Marcelin, having come over from Haiti, would also be present. "He's more difficult to negotiate than Phito, you know," Edmund said when we mentioned Pierre. "I met him in Haiti fifteen years ago. Usually he will speak nothing but French. Then he'll get tight and blast the United States in the clearest and most profuse English. Phito is the one of the two who has the birthright to *Thoby*, a distinguished lineage in Haiti. They had different mothers. They collaborate on their novels. Phito does all the creative side, the writing. Pierre does the research, works up the background; he's really an anthropologist. Phito has never been to a voodoo ceremonial in his life."

We had dinner in the same room of the Fort Schuyler where two months ago he had received the $5,000. The maître d' greeted him with the effusiveness to which he was accustomed. The last time I dined at the Fort Schuyler, Julio, a Spaniard and once the subject of a column of mine, had been on duty. Now our waiter was a man I had never seen before. His accent stamped him as from Utica's Little Italy. Edmund and he were clearly on terms of affection. Edmund took his hand, and I noticed that when the maître d' withdrew it there was a ten-dollar bill. As usual Edmund ate little. "I'm eating practically nothing these days," he said. He managed to make up the calories in whisky, three scotches, while continuing to freshen my martini glass.

"How is the Wells coming?" he asked. When I noted that Twayne was listing the title in its fall offerings, he asked that I be sure to have them send him a copy. "I still have the preface to that Russian edition you gave me, and I intend to translate the whole of it for you." This was in reference to a set of Wells's works, in Russian, that I had obtained two years ago from a dealer. "Moura Budberg—Countess of Budberg—is Wells's best translator, as well she might be. She was one of a succession of mistresses that plagued him throughout his middle age."[3] "Have you read *Apropos of Dolores*?" I asked. I explained that the novel, fairly late Wells, was plainly autobiographical. The heroine follows the pattern: continental courtesan hot on the trail of the writer hero. Edmund reminded me of his cutoff on Wells—1915 and *The Research Magnificent*—but he did not repeat the story of his disenchantment.

He asked me what degree I was working on. When I told him he said, "You ought to do your dissertation on Lowry." It was then I told him my goals: a thesis on *Under the Volcano* and a biography of Lowry. "But you should not do another Twayne. *I'm being done*, you know." More than a year ago, the last time we chatted, he had expressed what for him signified approval of a critical biography by Sherman Paul published by the University of Illinois Press. "It's not altogether bad, I think," he had said. On this occasion he spoke violently against it. "That fellow never attempted to reach me. His book is full of errors. I hope the Twayne is better, but I doubt it will be. I don't know who is doing it but whoever it is has not got in touch with me."

Mention of the Twayne books, which Wilson did not take seriously, moved him to talk about biography, which he did, and A. E. Hotchner's *Papa*, which had just been published. I mentioned a lecture I had heard by R. V. Cassill in which he denounced not only the evident betrayals by Hotchner but the publicity campaign which he said insured that a phony book *about* Hemingway was likely to sell better than any of the books *by* him. Edmund disagreed. "I don't see anything ethically wrong about what Hotchner did. Hemingway was a rather terrible person and competitive in the worst way. Did you know that he checked the all-time bestseller lists and never forgave Scribner's because *Gone with the Wind* outsold *For Whom the Bell Tolls*? That one did awfully well, too, by the way."

We left the Fort Schuyler at last and drove to my house. The Marcelins had already arrived—Phito, he of the gentle eyes and *sotto voce* tone, the dignity; Pierre, moustached and handsome, thickset and robust-looking, a contrast I had been prepared for by a snapshot taken with Malcolm Lowry, one I had duplicated at Vancouver. Edmund kissed the two women, Eva and Jo, embraced the men. They were old friends.

I should say something about Wilson and the brothers because, though his generous patronage of undiscovered writers was legendary, the case with the Marcelins was the only instance I know from firsthand. The politics and literature of Haiti became an overriding interest of Wilson's in the late 1940s. It may have been spurred by the formation of a UNESCO mission there which struck him as a concession that "capitalist" countries were willing to make in the direction of meeting a "socialist" country halfway. He tried unsuccessfully to convince *The New Yorker* to send him to Haiti to do the same sort of research as, fifteen years later, he would do in Eastern Canada. That Haiti was French rather than Spanish was all to the good. Ever since *Axel's Castle*, Wilson imagined himself a connoisseur of French poetry. As with any subject that engaged his attention, he read exhaustively. The collaborative fiction of the Marcelins gave him his best source material: *Canapé Vert* (1944), the prize-winning novel of the second Latin-American Literary Competition; *The Beast of the Haitian Hills* (1946); and a novel-in-progress, *All Men Are Mad*, about which he had heard and whose theme was bound to engross him, being a critique of morals which dramatizes the tension among the villagers between the national religion, Roman Catholicism, and voodoo and other tribal rites. Wilson met Philippe, on the recommendation of his friend Dawn Powell, when the Haitian came to Washington in 1948 as a translator for the Pan American Union. He found Phito's poems fascinating, like nothing he had ever read in French, and he tried, without success, to get them published in translation. In 1950, when *The Reporter* sent him to Haiti, he met Pierre, with whom, but only initially, he was more impressed. Wilson succeeded in assisting in the publication of *The Pencil of God* and in getting his own publisher to accept, although unfinished, the manuscript of *All Men Are Mad*, for which he would write an Introduction.

I make no pretense that I learned any of the above during the bibulous evening in our livingroom. It is mostly the counterpoint of Edmund's staccato—and inadequate—French playing harshly against Phito's whispered *français* that remains with me. Pierre drank more, spoke less, than the other two. I learned that Eva had consented to be translator for the work-in-progress. This especially pleased Edmund, I believe, because he considered Phito and Eva to be a unit in most things; now there would be an artistic union, too. But would she be able to translate the description of a voodoo ceremony, the cornerstone scene of the new book? To Edmund's question, Phito answered that if he, Phito, who had never seen the ritual either, could write about it from Pierre's notes, surely Eva could manage the admittedly further dilution of translation.

But, as I said, little of the conversation that evening intersected; it was *contrapuntal*, and only because Eva tossed us all lingual lifelines was there any communication at all. The two women talked about the house the Marcelins had bought in Cazenovia, one of my favorite villages Upstate (the other is Cooperstown). Cazenovia is bisected by U.S. Route 20, the nonpareil scenic route but one now regrettably pre-empted by the New York State Thruway. No expert in these matters, I believe I shall always regard U.S. 20, around Cazenovia, as the loveliest rural setting I have ever seen. Eva decided on it because she wished to be near her parents, living nearby in Canastota and both nearing ninety. She also worried about whether Phito, in frail health, could bear up under the Upstate winters and whether she could bear up under inactivity. Idleness made her restless—she had been away from her job as a U.S. Department of State art exhibits adviser for a year—and she thought she might like to teach again. She had also applied for a post with the New York State Council on the Arts and was to go to New York City next morning for an interview.

The union of Eva Ponticello of Canastota, New York—to me always ageless, a woman of the world to whom English had long ago reverted to second-language status, Italian being her third— and Philippe Thoby-Marcelin, voluntary exile from Duvalier's Haiti where his name, even during a quarter-century's absence, remained that of a leading poet in a country of poets, was a marvel in an age that is inhospitable to lasting marriages.[4]

At ten, the Marcelins prepared to depart. At the door, Eva asked Edmund to give Mary Pcolar their regards. "I'm helping to send her through college, and I haven't even slept with her," he replied in a way that I can only describe as non-boastful, kind.

Ten o'clock was also Edmund's time limit. He kissed Jo at the door. He struggled into my car for the long drive north.

Always, at a parting, he made plans for the next reunion. "When will you be free of that newspaper job so you can come to Talcottville?" But there would be only four days after my stint on the Utica *Daily Press* copydesk before Jo, Phil, and I would depart for my second year at Purdue. Edmund talked nearly the whole way about the old house and his determination never to allow it to pass hands in his lifetime. "Rosalind will inherit the place," he said. "You don't appear to know or care about such things, Dick, but the fact is that my life would have been altogether different if my mother had given me the house earlier. I'd have settled Upstate here as a landowner, a family man, and the entire direction of things would have been different."

I was not to see Edmund Wilson for a year. I left him remembering little things like the $10 tip at the Fort Schuyler and big things like his unqualified commitment to keeping up his house. All these testified to a clearer outlook, a factor of his recovered solvency, that had been missing on other occasions. I pondered his apparent regret in his old age at having been denied being a family man, and a landowner, up here in the country. If, early on, he had been gentry, how would his life have been different? Could ownership of land in his remote corner have quieted that restless intelligence that took the world for its province? And how for better? How better for the man who was the Sainte-Beuve of his time, "the moral and intellectual conscience of his generation," as Daniel Aaron put it in the Introduction to his *Letters*?[5]

For Wilson, age and infirmity impaired as no circumstances outside them ever had. They were forcing him into a night watch of unassuageable regret.

In an early short masterpiece ("The Door in the Wall"), H. G. Wells describes the life and death of a famous man who is besieged by hallucinative visions of an unfulfilled childhood to which they beckon return. Finally, at his pinnacle, Lionel Wallace enters a door in the wall to what he believes will be a garden but which is a careless trap that plunges him to his death. Wells ends the story on a question: Did *he* see it like that?

Did Edmund Wilson, approaching the end, see the urge to a gentle turning, for one such as he, unrealistically? The answer, perhaps, lies in the mordant tone of a poem, "Talcottville," he wrote that very year of 1966:

> You fade, old presences and leave me here
> In dimmer tuckle of a dismal May;
> I play old records and deal solitaire
> Through aimless hours of Memorial Day.

Cities I'll never see, books that I'll never read,
Magic I'll never master.
In a cage,
   I stalk from room to room
     lose heat and speed
Now entering the dark defile of age.[6]

Given that dark defile, could he any longer see his life as fulfilled, the way those who admired and loved him saw it?

Of Flattery's Lower Forms: Conrad Aiken

*T*HIS IS THE PLACE to recount my adventure—misadventure?—with the poet Conrad Aiken. Although Edmund Wilson figured tangentially, he did figure. I never told him the full story. I shall never know if he would have been amused or distressed.

During Easter week, 1967, to obtain an interview with the then seventy-seven-year-old Aiken, I armed myself, or so I thought, with what I thought would be a special inducement. In my naïveté, writing from Purdue, I asked Edmund Wilson, *my* Upstate neighbor, to write a supporting letter to Aiken, who had once been *his* neighbor at Brewster on the Cape. I was doing a paper for a Joyce seminar on the idea that Joyce had influenced Malcolm Lowry but had done so through a blood transfusion from his mentor Aiken.[1]

The timing seemed right. That January, in response to a *Times Literary Supplement* leader on Jonathan Cape's publication of *The Selected Letters of Malcolm Lowry*, Aiken spoke out on his younger contemporary with whom, in the thirties, he had joined in a remarkable literary and personal symbiosis.

"I have a favor to ask," I wrote to Edmund in early March. "I feel I must make an effort to talk to Conrad Aiken about Lowry. Aiken apparently has been inaccessible, at least on this topic, for years. As you know, he is approaching eighty. Do you feel (a) that a note from you would ease my way, and (b) that you would feel inclined to write such a note? . . . I'd like to go down to Savannah during our spring break for a chat with Aiken. What do you think?"

"I've been busy," Edmund responded. "Your letter to Aiken is all right, & I'll drop him a line right away."

Who was it who said that supporting letters are often the lowest form of flattery? I did not—fortunately, as things turned out—mention Wilson in my letter to Aiken. What I did not know, as I congratulated myself over the prompt invitation, was that Aiken would come armed with weapons brought to a fine sharpness by a half-century of defensive literary skirmishing. What I could not know, for Edmund and I had never discussed Aiken, was that the poet placed Wilson in the enemy camp.

I should have been forewarned, so badly did the interview start. I arrived in Savannah on Good Friday, but Aiken could not see me until Monday. Allen Tate, I. A. Richards, people like that, were in town for Easter. "Noontime sessions are best, if they suit you. Better give me a ring before you come, just to be sure." The voice on the phone combined traces of Southern aristocracy and Harvard.

When Monday finally came, the interview almost blew up before it started. The Aikens—he and "Lorelei Three" (third wife), the artist Mary Hoover—lived in a brick-stone Regency apartment, provided free of charge by Hy Sobiloff, a New York financier and sometime poet. I could not find the number—230 Oglethorpe East—so settled on the one between 228 and 232. I rang and waited. And waited. I assumed, after what seemed a quarter of an hour—it may have been ninety seconds—that I had better go by one of those hallway entrances that are shared by several apartments. I turned the knob; it was unlocked. I was standing in the Aiken parlor. There was no time to retreat. Glaring at me from the head of the staircase was an elderly man—heavyset, huge head, mandarin-looking, Charley Chan, without moustache.

"Are you in the habit of entering a man's house like a burglar?" That Harvard resonance again.

He gestured for me to ascend the stairs. I followed as he shuffled into a large drawingroom study. I noted a piano, tape recorder, microphone, all looking much used. Aiken hovered, not speaking, as I placed a stack of 4 × 6 file cards on the table. I removed from a briefcase the collected edition of his five novels, the collected poems, his ABC book of criticism, *Ushant,* copies of *Under the Volcano* and the Lowry *Letters,* the typescript of my essay which I had sent at his request.

"I guess I look like a book salesman," I said, trying for the lighter touch, "which is just about what I am."

"You wouldn't have needed that letter from Edmund Wilson," he said, the rich voice cracking at all the right places. "It was good to hear from him, but the fact is Edmund and I no longer have anything to say to each other. He's a social and political historian, not a literary critic. And he's very unreliable about poetry. One time he was sounding off on the *symbolistes.* I interrupted by questioning his reading of them. 'That's *irrevelant,* Conrad!' he shouted. 'Irrelevant maybe, Edmund, but not incompetent!'"

Aiken told of once suggesting a cartoon which would portray Wilson and Mary McCarthy, then recently divorced but still feuding, sitting opposite one another, each reading the other's latest diatribe. Aiken's suggested caption: *The Shock of Recognition.*

Two years after these talks,[2] I asked Wilson if he had seen an interview on Aiken's eightieth birthday—1969—in which Aiken cast Edmund as the exemplar of a general decline in taste. "Of course," Wilson replied, "and I sent him a 'cricket.'" A cricket, I learned, is a thing which the offended, in retaliation, slips inside a letter to the offender and which springs at him the moment the envelope is opened.

☙ VIII ❧

The Public Wilson

I DID NOT SEE EDMUND for fourteen months—that is, from late summer of 1966, when I returned to Purdue, until the fall of 1967, when I completed the residence requirement at Purdue and resumed teaching at Utica College. Through his Reporter-at-Large dispatches in *The New Yorker*, I was able to follow the quirky progress of the seventy-two-year-old Wilson on what was to be his last overseas journey.[1] Although there were stops in Jamaica, and in Paris and Rome, Edmund's destination was the Holy Lands to pursue and update his work on the Dead Sea scrolls.[2]

His petulance proceeded unchecked, whether he was reporting from the American School in Jordanian Jerusalem or the King David Hotel in Israeli Jerusalem. On the eve of his departure for Wellfleet, he received a phone call from the American consul in Tel Aviv warning that he should leave with the other Americans. Wilson complied, by implication, only because he had booked passage months before.[3]

I suppose, in Northrop Frye's formulation, Edmund Wilson would be classified as a *low-mimetic* writer: straightforward, unmetaphorical. Yet, for anyone who knew him well, countless passages from his travel writing become doubly vivid. En route to the airport at Tel Aviv, grateful, one would suppose, to be escaping the soon-to-be "1967 War," he can write:

I got up at five the next morning and was driven in a car to the airport. Riding along the roads that lead down from Jerusalem, whether in Israel or Jordan, is likely to be rather nerve-racking. The drivers dash around the loops, where one cannot see ahead what is coming, with a sheer unguarded drop at one side, and in Israel the driver, if one talks to him, is likely to gesticulate so wildly that one fears he may lose contact with the steering wheel.[4]

Reading a passage like that, for anyone who had driven Edmund up and down Deerfield Hill dozens of times without ever being able to relax him, makes such a driver wonder if setting had anything to do with his consternation.

Or, for one who listened with the sympathy one accords his elders as Edmund complained of motorcycles exhausting all night long or of jets breaking the sound barrier in their sonic zoom to Griffiss Air Force Base, this:

The airport gave the impression of a shelter for refugees fleeing from a hostile army. I have never, in a public place, heard such chattering, shrieking, uninhibited howling. The only people who seemed calm and quiet were an occasional old man with a bushy beard or one, shaved, with an open-necked shirt and a Ben-Gurion halo of graying hair fluffing out around his head. . . . The hysteria at the Air France bureau I attributed to Jewish excitement, but I found it much the same at Orly—the same confused officials, the same feverish checking and stamping, the same yelping of some French family whose arrangements were somehow not in order. When you find these two kinds of hysteria combined in the French-speaking officials waiting on French-speaking customers at the airport at Tel Aviv, you have something which makes getting a boarding pass a challenge to a war of nerves.
    It was a relief to board the plane. Once in the air, we travellers subsided.[5]

Just the other day, I read something that indicates the noisy distractions Wilson experienced on two continents, as well as at his home base, may have been comeuppance. A fellow *New Yorker* staffer writes that "some muting might have made more tolerable the shrill stabbing voice of Wilson-in-person, which, whenever the great man approached to within a hundred feet of where anyone else was trying to think, murdered cerebration."[6]

But that irony struck home much later. For then—summer 1967—as I read these septuagenarian quibbles, I found myself wondering: would he fasten his seatbelt when instructed, complain of air pockets, dress down Air France for serving champagne instead of Johnny Walker? *Stop the World*, the private Wilson demanded, even in public. *I want to get off.* Subside? Never.

Not even Talcottville, that summer of 1967, could shake him out of what his friends came to know as the "Hungarian sickness," a syndrome he called up often throughout the latter 1960s when his spirits and health were at low ebb. For the first time in the years I had known him, he returned to Wellfleet in early summer "rather glad of the pretext—to supervise the enlargement of my part of the house."[7]

I did not see him until October 19, the night of his first public appearance Upstate. This was Utica College's Harold Frederic symposium, an event Wilson and O'Donnell had had in preparation for a year. For one to whom any public lecture was a holy terror, Edmund displayed strong interest in the Harold Frederic celebration from the start.[8] Earlier, in letters to me at Purdue, O'Donnell had written that Edmund was actually the aggressor. Throughout the summer, he kept phoning Tom from Wellfleet and, weeks before the symposium, mailed a draft of his paper for Tom's approval. I had the impression Tom found it disappointing. "Good paper, of course, but nothing that Frederic people aren't already aware of."

Three Frederic scholars were to join Edmund on the stage of the Utica College auditorium. Besides O'Donnell, there were Professors Stanton Garner of Brown University and Austin Briggs, Jr., of Hamilton College. O'Donnell and Garner spoke on the early and late Frederic, of Utica/the Mohawk Valley and England/Ireland, respectively. Their papers were given at the opening session in late afternoon. That night, before what turned out to be the only full house I could recall for anything other than a film, Briggs spoke on "Harold Frederic and William Dean Howells." Edmund Wilson, anchor-man, spoke on "Harold Frederic, the Expanding Upstater." Almost three years later, *The New Yorker* finally published it under the same title as the second of two essays on "Neglected American Novelists."[9]

Jo, an admirer of *The Damnation of Theron Ware* (1896), generally considered Frederic's best novel, briefed me. Of that long evening, only one image remains vividly in memory: Wilson on the podium.

Tom wisely refrained from the long worshipful introduction that, in the presence of Edmund Wilson, the usual academic sycophant would have delivered. Instead, he expressed pleasure at being able to present "our neighbor from Talcottville, Edmund Wilson." That was all, and it was just right: the appropriate brevity, the *right sound*. I wish I could report that Edmund's performance had, too. Although there was no vocal giveaway—a tightening of the larynx—and although what E. J. Kahn, Jr., described as the "shrill stabbing voice" stayed well within bounds, Edmund was having a bad time of it. Head buried in script, he gripped the lectern as if it would at any moment slip from his hands. In forty-five minutes, he looked up from his paper four times—once to reel off the credits of his three co-panelists; once to make an insider's aside to O'Donnell about Celia Madden, the heroine of *Theron Ware*, and her walk-on role in a later novel ("I've always wondered, Tom, what happened to Celia between books"); and twice for even less memorable digressions.

"Read" papers, at best, are tough going, and few non-academic audiences are prepared for them. Edmund had told me in conversation that he had given up public lecturing because he could never make contact with his audience. On the night of his Upstate debut, his difficulty was painfully evident. The audience grew restive as the high-pitched drone varied only to accommodate an occasional fluff.

In common with many others who had driven to Utica from Talcottville, Boonville, Rome, Clinton, and Syracuse, Jo and I had an invitation, inscribed in Edmund's hand, to attend a reception at the Fort Schuyler after the symposium. For Edmund the party was a success. At no other time had so many of his Upstate friends gathered together under his auspices. Elena, who had driven him to Talcottville from Wellfleet a week before, was a gracious hostess, an imperceptibly aging woman with a rich low-register voice. The bar had been set up in the ladies' lounge, with the inevitable result that no one had elbow room to move around and it was impossible to hear what other people were saying.

On the attack against his *bête noire*, noise, Edmund, scotch in hand, shuffled to the larger cleared area and sat down. At last the bar was deserted. One could soon distinguish the intersecting conversations, less muffled in the larger room. Mary Pcolar, lovely and blonde in a dark frock, had been paired with Ivan Markí, who had left Hungary during the 1956 revolution and now taught American literature at Hamilton. Edmund had put Professor Markí's attractive French wife in touch with Phito Thoby-Marcelin, who was never at home in any other language.

A father looking after his own, Edmund beamed approval. I had only a few words with him, but they were memorable. He had received a copy of my book which had been published in May. He offered an unsolicited compliment: "Your Wells is good—I think it's very good—I want to talk to you about it. Can you join me for dinner Sunday—around six?"

One such as I, of limited visual sense, might forget October Upstate. Our last three—1967–69—loom especially beautiful in memory. They corresponded, also, to the changing color of my relationship with Edmund: the grayness of ceremony was by now mellowing to the comfortable greenery of friendship.

When Jo and I arrived at the old house on Sunday and knocked, we received no formal greeting. "Come in, the door's open." Edmund emerged in stocking-feet and stood at the entrance to his study. He announced that Elena had left that morning for Boston and Wellfleet. He would be leaving Tuesday by train for New York City "to see a friend's play." We learned later that the friend was Mike Nichols, who was directing a revival of *The Little Foxes*.

He was filled with the Frederic symposium and thought Utica College could do important things, culturally, for the community. He would like to be part of an annual symposium, one perhaps devoted to a different author each fall. I asked him if he would have accepted with the same readiness an invitation to speak at Harvard. "No, but then Harvard wouldn't make me a speaking offer," he replied.

Edmund mentioned for the first time that his Frederic paper, and a companion essay on another "neglected" American writer, Henry B. Fuller, were due out in *The New Yorker*. He proceeded, without the least prodding, to trace the genesis of his interest in Frederic and the history and literature of Upstate New York. "It all started when I got wind of an anthropologist named Lewis Henry Morgan. Morgan has written the best studies of the Iroquois; he lived in this vicinity—born in Aurora. Remarkable scholar and writer. My friend Bill Fenton of the New York State History Department in Albany knows more about the Iroquois than any living man. Now that he's got himself a grant, he'll be able to bring Morgan's work up to date."

It was not hard for Edmund, the most socially perceptive of people, to sense that all of these things were of limited interest to Jo and me. "Let's have a drink before dinner," he said. He walked to the back of the house, the kitchen; we could hear the tinkling of bottles. I looked at the paintings in the parlor, any of which an expert could place, I'm sure. It was obvious that none of them, nor any of the furniture, had been replaced since he inherited the house in 1951. Jo called my attention to a plate she had painted and given to him. It was hanging on the wall.

He returned with a fifth of Johnny Walker, then made a couple of fruitless trips back to the kitchen for soda water. After he had served us he went into his study across the hall from the parlor and returned with two books. I recognized my book along with Volume I of the fifteen-volume Russian edition of Wells's collected works.

Edmund raised his glass. For a moment I thought a toast was in the offing although I had never seen him do that. "If you don't mind, I'd like to read to you some of this from the Russian, and I'd better do it now before the whisky takes effect."

He proceeded to read for an hour and a quarter. Perhaps my most memorable picture of Edmund Wilson is of him adjusting his Benjamin Franklin spectacles and reading to us from the Russian original, fumbling skillfully for just the right words in English, trying to give us the impression his Russian was facile but instead creating the more compelling vignette of a busy man who had at some time during the past two years worked diligently over the translation so that he could now appear to be rattling it off. His reading style, even while groping for a phrase, was characteristically halting, little different, really, from his public-speaking style. Only once did he peer over the rimless glasses to assure himself of our attention. More commonly he would look to the wall for just the right word. My point in noting the sameness of the two manners is to show once again that he either lost awareness of his audience—any audience—or that he was giving in to his fears that any shift of gaze fron book to audience would be a ruinous distraction.

The passage was an interesting one. Kagarlitski, after tracing the history of Wells editions in the Soviet Union—here Wilson interpolated the information that Wells was popular there from *The Time Machine* (1895) on, [10] that his books have never been out of print—discusses Wells's first extended visit to the Soviets in 1920 and the disappointment of the literati over H. G. W.'s blimpy appearance. A seer should look like one. Kagarlitski recalled first-hand accounts of the stubby Englishman aboard a Russian train, equipped with portable tea brewer, his escort bodyguard, a mysterious sailor looking like a fugitive from Eisenstein's *Potemkin* (I noted that I had recently seen the old film again; Edmund corrected my pronunciation—*Poh-tyum-keen*). "Kagarlitski is implying—the year is 1934—that Wells was no more successful than other imaginative writers in probing the Russian state of mind." Edmund looked up, his new glasses providing the professorial touch. "Kagarlitski treats Wells's one book on the Soviet, *Russia in the Shadows* (1920), with more respect than he does any other Western critique. But, of course, we cannot overlook the remark about him, attributed to Lenin by Trotsky in 1920: 'Quel bourgeois!'"

I have always believed that Edmund would have gone on to translate the whole forty pages. My interruptions, however, slowed him down. Finally, at 7:30, he closed the book. Ought we not dine? While he was putting on his coat and helping Jo with hers, I took Edmund's copy of my book and wrote on the title page: "To my friend Edmund Wilson for pointing out to me the exact point where his disenchantment with Wells set in. In gratitude and affection . . ." I signed my name, the place, the date.

I handed him the book I had just inscribed. He opened it,

looked at the words, and proceeded to correct several citations that mentioned him. His only suggestions two years ago, when I had first shown him my notes, were to omit as irrelevant anything about the circumstances of our chats about Wells. Now he qualified his observation, quoted in the endnotes, that Wells and Shaw "were too Rousseauvian . . . for their novels and plays never go on to trace the outcome of the polygamous situations they herald. Many men and women of my generation saw in these books carte blanche for complete permissiveness and were irreparably damaged."[11]

He had not meant to include Shaw. "It was true of Wells, but Shaw was too Puritanical ever to suggest free love as a way of life. And I would never have said *permissive*. It is a word I have never used." And that reminded him. My style occasionally slipped into journalese. He had nothing against journalese in a newspaper but deplored it in literary material. "Of course, I've always insisted on being called a journalist—that's how I've earned a living—but I always tried to bring a literary style to my journalism."

Edmund knew of only one restaurant in the Talcottville area that would be open on a Sunday night. We would have to drive about five miles through country roads but roads which he, though a non-driver, knew well. The place was The Parquay, a diningroom attached to an inn, in Constableville. Our two young waitresses would not have been enthusiastic even if a tall man wearing a Western hat had appeared claiming he was LBJ. The kitchen was closed; we might have sandwiches. Edmund, voice rising, asked if the proprietor was working. A burly fellow with a Slavic accent emerged. Edmund talked to him briefly. Sandwiches it would be. He ordered three scotches.

The talk turned to Conrad Aiken. This was my first chance to tell about my Easter interviews in Savannah. Without mentioning Aiken's expressed distaste for his onetime Cape Cod neighbor, I made a brief and highly selective report.[12] He and Elena, he said, had avoided in late years what had once been annual visits to the Aikens in Brewster. "Conrad and Mary would invariably force their special martinis on us, and when we had to go to the bathroom we could never find it. If we finally did, we could never find our way back to the house."

Edmund was thoroughly familiar with the poems and stories and, although he had not read it through, Aiken's surrealistic autobiography *Ushant*. He had always thought the Aiken-Lowry relationship "sinister" and Aiken's feelings about his Harvard classmate T. S. Eliot "paranoid."

"Conrad Aiken is absolutely the most facile poet America has ever produced. He can churn out exceptional verse by the yard. I believe that is why Eliot was the greater poet. He had to work harder for his effects. But when he got them they were worth having."

He described Aiken as, like Hemingway, "terribly vulnerable" to what critics said. I had the feeling that he would not have said this if he didn't mean to imply that he, Wilson, was no longer much bothered by anything anyone wrote about *his* books,[13] or, for that matter, Aiken's caustic dismissals of him—even if I had had the courage, and I didn't—to tell him about them.

Edmund asked me how my book on Lowry was coming along. Did I have enough ready that he could direct to his publisher? I explained that I had already signed a second contract with Twayne; had done so, against his advice, because I am one of those writers who need contracts and deadlines to get anything done. I then told him, sparing details, of a prominent trade publisher whose editor, having liked several articles of mine on Lowry in *The Nation*,[14] asked if he might see my work-in-progress. After holding the manuscript for a year, he shipped it back. In the bottom of the box—deliberately?—was a letter from the reader. A few weeks later *Publishers Weekly* announced that the commercial house which had taken a year to turn down my manuscript had awarded a contract to the reader who had recommended rejection. "You were treated appallingly," Edmund declared, noting that the publisher in question had done one of his books. "But Roger Straus is above that sort of thing. He's the best publisher in America, a man who reads every book on his list and deeply cares about the writers under his imprint." It was a tribute Edmund obviously felt strongly enough about to repeat.

It was going on ten when we drove back to the old house. Edmund poured a nightcap. The subject turned to Svetlana Alliluyeva, the émigré daughter of Stalin. He was doing a long piece on her book but no interview. He expressed shock at the "vulgarity" of the English translation. He blamed the whole thing on the translator, a woman he described as "a newcomer to Russian." In the original, which he had read, Svetlana had done a straightforward, dignified book.

Edmund asked me to withdraw from the Utica College library the plays of Tolstoy. "I am working up Tolstoy for a book of my Russian writings." Much is lost in all the translations of the nineteenth-century Russians, especially of Tolstoy and *War and Peace*, he declared. "Even Constance Garnett was unable to convey Tolstoy's genius for *taking off* certain traits of speech, a dialect, a character's reversion to bad French. He gives us a whole world in a turn of phrase or a nuance of dialect." Was the Moncrieff translation of Proust not almost as good as the original? I had heard that it was. "No, Moncrieff misses the *longueurs*, the incredible lassitude of Proust's speech."

Two years before Edmund, deep in his cups, had read aloud to us "The Guerdon," a Beerbohm parody of Henry James. He presented me that evening Sir Max's *A Variety of Things*, from which "The Guerdon" was drawn. Reading to Jo and me at the close of an evening at the old house was to become a tradition. He had been enjoying, he said, Edward Marsh's memoirs—"better even than Swinnerton's." He began reading, with obvious relish, a superb parody of Milton's epic style, a description of Adam and Eve's toothbrushing habits. He read with *sprezzatura*. Later, Jo and I said—neither of us prompting the other—that we wished Edmund could have done the same in reading "The Expanding Upstater" just ten days ago.

Edmund looked exhausted as he finished. It was nearly 10:30. With encouragement, I believe he would have stayed up all night with us. At the door, as always, he kissed Jo. She remarked how much fitter he looked than fifteen months ago. He always warmed to concern about his health. "Uh, uh, yes, I suppose I am better, but not the way I'd like. I have angina and the gout, you know; have had for years." I told him that I had suffered two kidney stone attacks at Purdue and that lately I had been on what my doctor described as a gout diet. "If you have the gout, I can fix you up. Nothing to do with eating. Largely hereditary, you know." I had the feeling that even in his ailments Edmund Wilson wished to pay homage to his ancestors.

He spoke of how difficult it had become to accustom himself to limiting his activity to short walks. "Old age has its compensations. Less anxiety about what I'm going to write—especially mornings. But I miss swimming and all those things I can't any longer do. I dwell on old love affairs. I find it hard to accept that I'm old."

We stood in the entrance. He did not accompany us, as he had always done before, when we walked to the car. I heard the sound of the door closing, saw the porch light go out even before we reached the car.

Pastoral and Polemic

NO ONE TO MY KNOWLEDGE has ever sought to formulate Edmund Wilson as a regionalist. "If Wilson is to be categorized as a critic," writes Harry Levin in a review of the *Letters,* "it must be as a critic at large, a critic of everything."[1] Yet his Upstate persona is that of a "neighbor" with a regional constituency for which he felt the urges of the schoolmaster who is also the patron.

More than a year before the Frederic symposium, he observed in his diary a sense of "cultural explosion in this 'area.'" This explosion he sees as a national phenomenon "*pari passu* with delinquency and crime [and] partly due to federal handouts and foundation grants."[2] He reflects a characteristic skepticism over government-sponsored attempts at cross-fertilization in the arts. He writes of turning away two young men who sought his cooperation in a proposal for a government-subsidized summer school at Leonardsville where "people in the different arts [would] be able to talk to one another; [where] some more or less distinguished person [could] come . . . to read a paper or speak—to be followed, of course, by discussion." It would not work, Wilson argues. "For a painter or a writer to talk to a musician . . . was like a carpenter talking to a plumber. What a person practicing one art can get from someone practicing another must come from experiencing the other's work."

Wilson goes on to explain *his* notion for community education, a kind of annual regional workshop intended to inform Upstaters about what there is of their local culture that they know nothing about. His list of informing topics provides clues to the interests of a man who, in old age, was trying to *learn* the region of his forebears with the same dedication he gave the Civil War or the scrolls from the Dead Sea: Harold Frederic; Lewis Morgan; Samantha and the Widow Bedott; Philander Deming, a short-story writer and "discovery" of Tom O'Donnell's; local artists such as Arthur Davies, William Palmer, and Henry DiSpirito; the Oneida Community.

Spurred on by the publication of my book on H. G. Wells, I wrote Edmund in February about the possibility of his participating in a Utica College symposium on Wells. My book's publication was followed by *The Future As Nightmare: H. G. Wells and the Anti-Utopians*, by Mark R. Hillegas, whom I came to know when he was teaching at Colgate in the early sixties. After decades of neglect, a coterie of critics—Colin Wilson, Bernard Bergonzi, and David Lodge in England; Hillegas, Anthony West, and Robert P. Weeks in the U.S.—had been reassessing the earlier works of Wells, especially the scientific romances, and finding that at their core they imaginatively project a deep cosmic pessimism. Why not bring together some of these Wellsians to chart the resurgence of the old scientific romancer—all of them and Edmund Wilson, too? Jo, wise as always, cautioned me against getting my hopes up. She knew. When Edmund agreed to lecture at—in fact, spearheaded—the Harold Frederic celebration last year and this year was talking of participation in a session on the Iroquois, he came to Utica College as a regionalist, an Upstate neighbor, not as a world figure. Jo predicted that he would refuse to have anything to do with a public seminar on anything but Upstate materials, and she was right. His letter of refusal was humane; it contained a promise to make his annual appearance "in the country" earlier than usual—in April.

He arrived, in fact, on May 9. Mary Pcolar met him at Hancock Airport in Syracuse. Although we knew he had arrived, Jo and I waited for *him* to call. He did, three weeks later. He had been "galavanting," he told us, to see Reuel, his daughter-in-law Marcia, and their baby—this in Chicago; to see some plays in New

York, a city of disenchantment and filth and "young people as to whom you couldn't tell whether they were pimps and prostitutes or simply hipsters and swingers."[3] But by mid-June he had settled in at the old house for the next four months. From all accounts—his diary entries in *Upstate* added to my memories of our encounters—summer 1968 may have been the happiest of his old age (he had just turned seventy-three). "This summer has so far, I think, been the pleasantest I have spent up here. . . . People have asked me out a lot, and sometimes I have had to refuse in order to get an evening to myself. The weather has been mostly delightful. I am becoming more involved in the community. . . . Bob Weiler's gardening has very much improved the whole place. The white rose by the front porch, which my mother called 'Aunt Lin's,' has begun blooming again." And the showy Ladyslippers, which he considered "exquisite independent beings," bared their secrets to him, became touchstones for the idyll, the late dividend, of those years.

Perhaps it is not for me to say, who knew him only at the end of his life, but I cannot help but think that it was in his seventies that Edmund came closest to breaking out of what Alfred Kazin called his fate of being "sentenced to the sentence." Joseph Epstein puts the matter differently when he writes of Wilson's "second adolescence in the 1960s."[4] What Edmund rarely articulated in conversation, but what he manifested in noble efforts at accessibility Upstate, was an attempt to deal with the other claims of his personality: his absorption with the people who were his forebears and, above all, his desire for human links. Although it was true, as Epstein goes on to note, that his bookishness was also his salvation, it was Wilson's sense of community that tempered his bookishness and enriched our lives.

What these neighborly recollections may not show—possibly *cannot* show, in the unstated way they developed—was the mellowing in *our* attitudes, Jo's and mine, as we prepared on a Friday in early June for the annual renewal. Conversation, we could now anticipate, would be a series of reminders. What we now had was a kind of verbal shorthand, truncated, often allusive responses, residue from other conversations.

He was fuller of the summer's projects than I had ever seen

him. There was, of course, the work on *The Dead Sea Scrolls*. Yet all this—all his major work—was being set aside by something else which he talked about with fervor.

"I'm working on something that will blow the lid off the MLA and the whole American Literature racket," he declared. Then he frustrated us, at first, by declining to go into any details. "It's all too complicated." We really didn't need any details. His thrust was contained in a letter to the *New York Review of Books*, dated March 14, 1968, in which he at once took the side of Lewis Mumford against a new edition of the papers of Emerson and lashed out at the "academic racket that is coming between [classical American writers] and the public to which they ought to be accessible."

This is not the place to discuss in detail what was to become Wilson's second polemic of those years. The first led to the futile *Cold War and the Income Tax* in which he struck out at favorite targets, the U.S. bureaucracy and the Defense establishment, but barely acknowledged that most of his troubles were brought on by his carelessness in neglecting to file returns after the death of his attorney. Wilfrid Sheed, a devoted friend writing for the one Catholic journal Wilson admired, found *The Cold War* "an extraordinarily disappointing book . . . mostly a narrow peevishness. . . . This is Mr. Wilson, the country squire, brandishing his cane at the urchins and muttering to himself, like W. C. Fields, about his ineffable woes."[5] The best parts of the pamphlet were those in which the quintessential "professional" chronicled his struggle to stay afloat: a grand old man of letters who, at seventy-four, was unwilling, according to Charles P. Frank, "to withdraw into the shrine of the guest lecture, the symposium, or the graduate seminar to be treated with reverence by polite students."[6]

Now with apparent glee, whether intentionally or not, Edmund was making me a sounding board for another broadside, one already launched in print, against the Modern Language Association. Edmund had got it into his head that the efforts of some sort of lobby of the MLA had deflected National Endowment for the Humanities funds from one of his cherished projects to a bastardized version being mounted by the literature academics. He had spoken as early as our first meeting in 1963 of the desirability for the general reader of easily accessible editions of out-of-print

American classics. He had nurtured a dream of a series of beautifully printed and produced thin-paper volumes à la the French *Editions de la Pleiades*. Now, just when he thought the NEH had been primed by *his* friends in high publishing places, the money had somehow been "whisked away" by *their* friends. "The MLA had . . . a project of its own for reprinting the American classics and . . . had ours suppressed," he had written that spring.[7]

"My pamphlet will take on the whole American Literature gang, and I'll be curious to know what someone like you, about to be Ph.D.-ed, thinks of it." He spoke the words in that high-pitched, dialectical-imperative voice that signaled something was on his mind that pre-empted solicitude. From such intimidating beginnings were co-conspirators enlisted. "I've been talking to Tom O'Donnell, and he agrees with me. His backing means something. He's in on the racket although with some reluctance, I take it. Cady [Professor Edwin H.] of Indiana has assigned Tom to do an edition of William Dean Howells' poems. Howells' poems! Who can *read* them?"

Edmund's voice always soared when derision was on the way. He declared that his broom would sweep in nearly everybody who, as the expression has it, was "in on the take." Edmund reserved for special villainy the distinguished Shakespearean bibliographer and textualist, Professor Fredson Bowers of the University of Virginia.

"I visit Charlottesville from time to time—the least changed city in America—and I am on friendly terms with Fredson Bowers," Edmund said. "His seminars on bibliography are undoubtedly wonderful. It takes a special intelligence to do that sort of thing well. But to make a bibliographer the master hand, as he apparently is, behind the whole MLA boondoggle shows to what depths these editions have sunk. It's all nit-picking trying to disguise itself as literary scholarship. And I have no reason to believe that the Fredson Bowerses are much interested in literature at all."

Edmund went on to describe for us the thrust of *The Fruits of the MLA*. The pamphlet was to appear early in the fall—two installments in *NYRB*, plus a section devoted to the expected deluge of letters, pro and con. His attack would be *Swiftian*, Wilson said in a self-congratulatory mood that was not his characteristic grain. It would demonstrate that the new editions, with their heavy baggage of unnecessary annotation and other ponderous apparatus, done up in books that were too large and heavy to hold and their type set in lines too wide for the eye to travel without effort, were finally unreadable.[8]

Rereading *The Fruits of the MLA* after a decade, I still chuckled over many of Wilson's examples of elephantine academic marshalling to the picking up of peas. Anyone who has gone through graduate studies in literature at any American university since the war cannot but join Wilson's bemusement, for all its disingenuousness, over, for example, the MLA volume of Melville's *Typee* whose credits list three editors, a "Bibliographic Associate," and a "Contributor of the Historical Note." For Wilson the project is "so relentlessly carried out in the technical language of this species of scholarship . . . that a glossary should be provided for readers who are not registered union members . . . of the Modern Language Association." A few lines later he purports to wonder why an anthropologist was not consulted to help Professor Leon Howard sort out the interesting possibilities of how much of *Typee* is documentary, based on Melville's experiences, and how much the play of invention and imagination. "One could not," he concludes, "expect that the MLA would care to humiliate its Hinman Collating Machine by associating it with a raw anthropologist."

The verve with which Wilson sought to demolish academic scholarship is a species of the same disdain that lay behind his unproduced *furkin* play about the Elizabethan scholar and his pirated edition of an obscure play. *The Fruits of the MLA* is as amusing for haters of the proliferation that passes for scholarship among some English academics as *The Cold War and the Income Tax* is reinforcing for some enemies of the IRS, but neither pamphlet proved to be useful at the level Edmund Wilson presented it.

What commends Wilson's literary criticism—or any of his major nonfiction texts, for that matter—is the evidence that they have been *distilled*. Works like *Axel's Castle* and *The Wound and the Bow* plunge with journalistic directness to the heart of their matters. A sensibility free of cant and the circuitous dodge leads his reader along a path that is paved with common sense and that marvelous sort of joint discovery that occasionally unites serious reader with serious scholar.

Wilson was more of a public teacher than any of the professional pedagogue-scholars of the Academy. His rage for readable new texts for the educated general reader fell within that calling. His manner was blunt yet conversational, his intent always clear. Thinking of Wilson, V. S. Pritchett notes of the "new man," the successor in ours to the classic man of letters of the eighteenth century, that "he had to increase his range yet come brusquely to the point."[9]

That "community of scholars" at whose subsidized industry Wilson shook his fist in the summer of 1968 constitutes a different breed altogether; they are, by training and, often, inclination, unlikely in their endeavors to come brusquely to the point.

Many first books for academicians emerge from doctoral dissertations. They reflect the premium that is placed in graduate study on exemplification and attribution. Hence they are often loaded with the explicit scholarly apparatus Edmund Wilson decried. Most good dissertations are of little interest to the literate, well-read generalist. That reader may well come upon a book by Edmund Wilson and delve into it because it makes its point quickly and cogently. In its inexorable progress to the university library, the refurbished dissertation rarely reaches the reader of Wilson. It will rest, unread, until a subsequent Ph. D. candidate, encouraged to specialize, is directed by his adviser not to overlook that new work of scholarship.

I have known a number of poets who found Wilson's readings of, say, the symbolists, unreliable—Conrad Aiken and Philippe Thoby-Marcelin, for example. I know of no teacher of literature who has not found much to admire in Wilson's criticism. The tribute most often voiced is on the galvanism of his style, the mastery of the periodic sentence, to whose accomplishment he once, only partly in jest, credited his success.

On that June Friday, I said nothing that resembled any of the above. To Edmund's tirade against the MLA, I wanted to say—but didn't—that many of its members I knew to be staunch admirers of his. I wanted to say that a book like Maurice Beebe's *Ivory Towers and Sacred Founts* seemed to me to owe a lot to Wilson; to be, in fact, a kind of undistilled *Axel's Castle* and that he ought to read it. I wanted to tell him, in detail, how many of my mentors at Purdue, with national reputations in their scholarly fields, had pressed me to chat with them about Edmund Wilson; how an especially august one had confessed that he had tried to model his own style on Wilson's.

Instead, I was relieved when he moved from the MLA to the safer ground of *The New Yorker*. He had made a rare extended visit to that magazine's offices just before coming Upstate. Did he still know the people there? "Since the passing of the Algonquin crew—Benchley, Thurber, Dorothy Parker, and so on—it has become an article of faith for no one to know anybody else." He described Penelope Gilliatt, the film critic, as "the most interesting" of the newcomers. She had "that kind of flaming red hair that you know is real" and he had been "trying to get her up here—so far unsuccessfully." I did not quite know what to make of that. Did Edmund want her to inscribe something on one of his windows? At that moment, I remembered something Eva Thoby-Marcelin reported having heard Katherine Ann Porter say in conversation about the younger Wilson. With females, especially the sort who write poems, he was "like a fox in a wheat field with a flaming tail."

"*The New Yorker* has all this money, Edmund was saying, "and some of us are making a living from it, including me." It was as if he thought it did not matter if anyone at the magazine talked to you as long as the payments kept coming. He expressed annoyance at the continued delay in the appearance of his piece on Harold Frederic. "It is so un-topical that it baffles them. I had to threaten to submit it to the *New York Review of Books* in order to get a commitment."

He was reading, he went on, his friend V. S. Pritchett's memoir, *The Cab at the Door*, which he recommended to me. "Pritchett had a childhood that had a lot in common with Wells's, and his book is in the spirit of Wells's autobiography[10] though, from start to finish, a more artistic work, a gem."

That summer I had published a paper on Richardson's *Pamela*[11] and was surprised when Edmund told me he had never read it. "I once tried *Clarissa* though." He had read Fielding as a schoolboy and written a parody of him. He liked Sterne and Smollett, but the fiction of the eighteenth century was generally not to his taste. "I've missed a lot of things," he volunteered. He did not read *New Yorker* fiction as a rule; "Elena tells me what's worth looking at."

Something steered us onto the topic of actresses. He asked us to guess which film actress he found "irresistibly attractive." My guess was Katherine Hepburn, Jo's was Sophia Loren. "Neither," he answered. "It's Doris Day. So much the true female." He said he had begun to like movies and mentioned for the first time having seen *The Yellow Submarine,* of which I shall have more to say later.

Edmund had been in France, Italy, and Hungary last year en route to Israel. He said that he preferred Italian and Hungarian women. All his life he had been wary of Frenchwomen. Elena, he told us, is middle-European. "We have been married twenty-two years. She has kept my family together when things could have gone to pot. All my children absolutely adore her. With Elena, family is everything. I owe her very much." He spoke with pleasure of his spring visit with Reuel, who taught Slavic languages at the University of Chicago, the same school where Edmund briefly lectured in 1939. Rosalind was expected later in the summer. Helen was "jumping from job to job in New York. She dropped out of Barnard, you know."

As usual, the pint of Johnny Walker ran out quickly, and it was only seven o'clock. The doorbell rang. It was a delivery from the Boonville liquor store. "I've been going through a bottle a night. Different bottle. Different friends. Every night. But I've got to get back to the Dead Sea scrolls."

Mabel Hutchins had arrived just before the delivery boy. She cooked us a superb filet mignon with vegetables done to perfection. "I don't vouch for the wine. I got it at the supermarket." As usual, he picked over the food. We talked about Eva and Phito and their apparent permanent residency Upstate. "She has got Phito out of drinking. No one but a Sicilian could have done it." Now Eva needed a full-time position, and would we speak to Tom O'Donnell about "something in French," a language in which Eva had, Edmund stressed, both a conversationalist's and a translator's fluency? Eva, I said, was the best-looking older woman I had ever seen. He beamed approval.

Edmund planned to return Upstate in mid-October for his second Utica College symposium, this one on the Iroquois. "My part will consist entirely of reading an excerpt from my book.[12] The chapter on the Little Water Ceremony. I'm always reworking old material." Earlier he scoffed at my referring to him as a book-a-year man. He did not scoff at the idea of a symposium-a-year.

Going on ten—we had arrived at six—it was clear that he was fatigued. "Yes, grandpa's getting tired." It was the first time we had heard him refer to himself that way. Wasn't it appropriate, Reuel and Marcia having recently made him a grandfather for the first time? He kissed Jo, as always. After a promise to get together later in the summer, we inched toward the door. Edmund came outside with us, stood on the porch and watched us off as, until last summer, he had always done.

A Woman's View

IN "THE HOME PLACE," I noted that Jo's being a native of the region and my being an outsider lent balance and variety to our conversations with Edmund Wilson. If these recollections so far have seemed weighted toward Wilson the literary man, it may be because I have not given Jo's contributions the importance they deserve. She reached him at levels that drew out traits and tendencies I would have missed altogether. In the years we knew him he preferred the company of women.

Edmund's promised reunion "later in the summer" proved to be early in the fall, in October, about ten days after he came up from Boston to participate in a symposium on the Iroquois at Utica College.

Edmund warned us that he was having a terrible bout with shingles and we would have to make allowances. He phoned Saturday morning to invite us for dinner at the old house. He had wanted to see us the previous week, had driven to Utica with Mary, but returned almost immediately in a state of exhaustion. Could we make it for Tuesday, around six? His voice sounded worn.

It was always difficult for us to gauge the long drive north. Edmund always expressed his concern that we may have got lost or had an accident. He showed no ill effects of the shingles, seemed pleased we were on time. He moved us quickly into his sitting-room but not until he had demonstrated his old style courtliness. How charming it was when he would rush to Jo's side to remove her coat before we got inside the door. I can still hear his voice: "H-h-here, here, let me do that."

The pint of Johnny Walker Red, three glasses, a bowl of ice cubes, a pitcher of water—all in readiness. I had the feeling that waiting until six may have required mind over matter.

His first remark, after he had poured half a water-glass of scotch for each of us, was: "Jo, you've done something to your hair. I like it, very becoming." Recently she had had her hair tinted blonde, cut short, and combed into bangs. "The TV commercials all say blondes have more fun; I thought I'd try and find out if this would be true for me." Edmund laughed more broadly than usual and fired back something about my having to keep a watch on Jo and too bad he wasn't younger.

We had hardly begun our drinks when the doorbell sounded. Edmund was upstairs looking for a book. Jo called to him, "Are you expecting visitors?" He appeared at the head of the stairs, flustered, as if he had suddenly remembered something. "It must be the O'Donnells, but I'm sure I made that date with them for later in the week. (The symposium on the Iroquois was the 17th, nine days off.)

Sure enough, it was Tom and Gert. As it turned out, they had also made a date. *They* were to take *him* to dinner. *He* was to have *us* to dinner. Same day, same time. True, Edmund had explained a change of plans but not one as yet involving the O'Donnells. Mabel Hutchins had come down with the flu; we would go out to dinner instead: the Parquay in Constableville. Edmund was perturbed, visibly. He liked both couples, but I think he preferred us separately. With Tom, conversation would revolve around Upstate history and literature; with us, Edmund was not prospecting: anecdotes, reminiscences, his current writings, the importance of putting down roots, almost anything. We always liked it when he would pull up short and remind us never to repeat this or that.

The subject of the Iroquois, which may have been on Edmund's mind when he made the date with the O'Donnells, was not to occupy us this time. As soon as we were seated at the Parquay, he said to Tom, "Can you come up some afternoon this week so we can discuss the lecture?" That matter settled, Edmund announced that somebody would have to drive him to Utica after dinner. With Mrs. Hutchins ill, he would stay at the Fort Schuyler for two days, until Thursday, when Elena would arrive and they would return to the old house. He could no longer manage alone. But it was mostly in consideration of his ailing housekeeper. She would worry, he said, and try to come by; he thought that only if the house was empty would she stay in bed. There was no food in the house; all he had eaten the whole day was peanut brittle. How could Edmund have drunk two tumblers of scotch on an empty stomach and shown no effects? All he ate for dinner was a fried egg sandwich—that and a double scotch. The four of us must have struck him as gluttons with our plates of prime ribs. However, Edmund was not the ascetic of the dinner table. He never passed up dessert, loved creamy cakes and all flavors of ice cream. I recall him eating two helpings of Boston cream pie one night at our house after having toyed with the steak. This time he ordered a hot fudge sundae and all but ate the cup it came in.

Edmund, as usual, insisted on paying the check. Tom protested: this was not the plan; he was to be their guest. We offered to split the tab. Edmund, for the only time I can remember, agreed.

It was an evening of awkwardnesses of the kind we thought well behind us in our relationship with Edmund. There was also a small embarrassment that later came to loom large. Tom and Edmund, despite the earlier injunction against the Iroquois as dinner subject-matter, began, in effect, to rehearse their forthcoming lectures. Tom made a reference to the novels of Wilson's Boonville neighbor, Walter D. Edmonds. Wilson expressed concern over Edmonds' latest, *The Musket and the Cross*, which he described as "a straightforward historical work" on the author's favorite landscape, Upstate New York. "The historians," he said, "are unlikely to take into account that Walter Edmonds is a novelist writing history. I'm afraid they'll clobber him." Wilson's voice rose as it always did when he was offering strong criticism of a work. And, as it turned out (although we didn't know it at the time) someone *did hear* the remarks about Walter Edmonds: the man himself! As Edmund droned on, oblivious of anyone, a couple passed our table. The man smiled at Jo and said good-evening. I noted she smiled back and said hello. As they worked their way to the back, I tried to remember where I had seen the man. Wilson's back was toward the newcomers and he did not immediately notice them.

While coffee was being served, our non-coffee-drinking host had time to take in his surroundings. I could see his eyes resting, although a bit uncertainly, on the couple who had just entered. "I think it's my friend Walter Edmonds," he said, uncharacteristically *sotto voce*. "I hope he didn't hear our conversation." He rose and walked to the table occupied by the Edmondses. I heard him say, "How nice to see you. We were just talking about you, Walter. Did you hear?" "No," his reply was distinct, "and I'm glad I didn't." The exchange could not have sounded more friendly. I recalled the meeting two years earlier—our encounter in the Wilson vestibule, Walter Edmonds having dropped by to pick up *Mostly Canallers*. "We must get together soon, for I won't be up here after next week." "Remember us to Elena."

Once outside, the O'Donnells said goodnight; Tom and Edmund made a date to discuss the symposium; and Edmund joined us in our car. We stopped at the house to pick up Edmund's valise in which, along with a change of clothing and toilet articles, he had placed the fifth of Johnny Walker Red which we had brought for him. We always wondered why one so generous always bought his scotch by the pint. Edmund alone could drink that much in an evening and frequently did. Was the short supply deliberate, a prodding of prudence, so as to hold back himself while leaving enough for his guests? Edmund was as delighted with the gift as a child with a piece of candy.

While we drove down to Utica, Jo asked Edmund what he planned to do in Utica, alone and with two days on his hands. She reminded him that she wasn't teaching that autumn, that Philip was a high school freshman, and that she would be at his service as a driver. Any errands, shopping, business to look after? "That's perfectly wonderful, Jo," he said. "As a matter of fact, I have some shopping to do. *Would* you go with me, Jo?" She could not imagine what kind of shopping he would be doing, but whatever it was she would be a willing companion. "Could you join me for lunch tomorrow—at the Club? Good. We'll plan on meeting there early, say at 12:30, and do the town."

It was 10 P.M. when we pulled up in front of the Fort Schuyler. We were sure, remembering how tiring he had found his last drive to Utica, he would be ready for bed. To our surprise, he insisted that he and Jo get out while I parked the car. As I entered the Club, I saw them being greeted by a man I had never seen before, a rather husky blond fellow who asked if he could be of help. He had what I took to be a German accent. "You're new here, aren't you?" asked Edmund. Before the man could reply, he added, "I'm Edmund Wilson. I have a reservation for tonight." It was obvious to me that the man, who was Charles Helmsing, the new manager, had been waiting all evening for just this arrival and now was upset at the sight of a woman late at night in a club exclusively for males.[1]

Charles Helmsing tended bar for us, served a nightcap— scotch, of course. It was nearly midnight when we arrived home. I had an early class. Jo was looking forward to a shopping expedition with a man who, in her opinion at least, appeared to need everything.

They were lucky in the weather: one of those days in early autumn that are unmatched anywhere, with the sun shining and the maples holding their leaves, riotous with color, despite late-September frosts. Jo was exuberant that morning, a day made for walking; but, at the noon hour, the traffic on Genesee Street would be predictably heavy. She had difficulty finding parking and arrived ten minutes late. There he was, she told me, looking as we will always remember him, watching through the picture window, the aristocratic nose sniffing out arrivals, his eyes darting from the pages of the *Watertown Times*. I asked Jo what lunch at the Fort Schuyler was like.

"Edmund guided me past the for-men-only reading lounge to the dining room. He was in a jovial mood. 'Shall we celebrate with a drink first?' The question was rhetorical. He ordered a vodka martini and expressed disappointment when I asked for scotch and water. 'Remember, I'm driving,' I said, all the while wondering where he did his shopping and for what. I should stop worrying, he assured me. We were going to *walk* to the Boston Store, the one large department store in Utica that had so far resisted joining the mass exodus to the suburbs[2] and 'where I can find everything I want under one roof.'

"Then—I should not have been surprised but I was—he proposed another drink. 'You'll join me for a martini, won't you?' Who was I to put a damper on the best mood I had ever seen him in? The conversation turned to you: the difficulty of writing a dissertation while teaching four courses and serving on committees that were formed almost daily in those days as holding actions against threats of student revolts. 'The trouble with Dick is he's too easy, too soft. He hasn't learned to say no. Writers go into teaching in order to write, and then they don't write. Did you know that Vladimir Nabokov, who taught for a time at Cornell, was grading all of those student papers himself and getting none of his own work done at all? Some of us had to lodge protests on his behalf.'"

Jo did not then know about the Nabokov-Wilson feud over Nabokov's translation of Pushkin, and Edmund did not talk about it. However, mention of Nabokov may have triggered discussion of another celebrated Russian émigré, Svetlana Alliluyeva. She had been a guest at the house in Wellfleet, a charming and attractive woman. Earlier he had told us of his conviction that she had literary ability of a high order. "Don't judge Svetlana by her first book," he told Jo that afternoon.[3] "The translation was terrible, *simply terrible*, by a woman who had no literary sense at all. Svetlana is made to sound colloquial and inaccurate where, if you read her in the original Russian, she is dignified and perfectly clear. The book she is working on now will be of major importance.[4] I'm afraid it may get her into trouble because she spares no one. The translation will be by an expert. It will make a good deal of difference. So far she has been entirely misunderstood over here."

Jo did not have to tell me about her anxiety about whether they would ever make it through lunch. "Dick, one more drink and I knew there would be no shopping. 'I think we'd better eat,' I said. He ordered, of all things, a fried egg and ignored the menu with its delightful choices. Over my protests, he ordered a half bottle of wine. 'It's not every day I get to have a beautiful woman to myself to do the town,' he said in that laughing way he had that was something between a chuckle and a huff. 'You know, you *are* a beautiful woman, the best of the Italian type.' Now I was flustered but for a different reason. *Beautiful* is never a word anyone ever

applies to me. How could anyone resist such flattery? Much as I
didn't want to acknowledge it, Edmund was in his cups."

By the time they had finished eating, some of the glow had
dulled. "No coffee for me, but bring some for the lady and a
chocolate sundae for me." He could not understand how Jo could
pass up dessert. Jo's eye was ever on the clock—now 2 P.M. "I
realized I still had no idea what we were going shopping for or how
long it might take us. Remember, Dick, I was to pick up Philip at
Utica Free Academy at 4:30; Edmund was to get a nap at the Club
before you were to bring him home to dinner."

Then Edmund touched on a subject of special interest to
Jo. Some months ago I had mentioned to him that she had written
what I thought to be a compelling short story.[5] To my surprise—
more so Jo's—Edmund remembered. "Dick tells me you've written a very good short story. I'd like to read it. Will you send it to
me or give me a copy?" "I will some time," Jo said, trying to avoid
the false modesty we knew Edmund detested but all the while
thinking that by tomorrow he would have forgotten all about the
story. At last he signed the check, bade her wait for him while he
went to the cloakroom. Jo was surprised when he returned without
his tattered raincoat, something he wore rain or shine, and, most of
all, without his walking-stick. We had rarely seen him without it,
the past year or so, especially on any occasion requiring walking.
Perhaps he wanted as few reminders as possible that he was seventy-three, subject to the gout, and other than a still-vigorous man
who would rather walk than ride. Besides, he was out with a young
woman, out to do the town. Canes were symbols of infirmity.
Fortunately, the Boston Store was four blocks from the Club, all
downhill. It was the walk back that worried Jo.

Jo noted a perkiness in his gait, something that he could
muster up for any occasion that was to be *his* show.

"Dick," she said, "he proceeded to walk briskly ahead of
me. It was as if I was not accompanying him at all; as if he was
leading a stranger to places unknown. From two paces behind him,
I called, 'What are we going to buy?' He turned around, as if
suddenly remembering he had a companion. 'I need some things
for the house, some sheets for when Elena comes, a shade for the
lamp by my bed. Mrs. Hutchins says the one on it now doesn't give
off enough light because it's cardboard. Bad for my eyes, you

know. And tennis shoes. I'll need those for the picnic with Mary [Pcolar] and her family and our walk down by Sugar Creek next week. I'm very much looking forward to that. It's been many years since I walked along the creek, a place I loved as a boy.' Tennis shoes—for Edmund Wilson? Any thoughts I may have entertained of helping select a new raincoat or hat had now been dispelled.

"As we made our way downtown, several acquaintances stopped to say hello, exchange a few words. I thought Edmund was unaware of these interruptions, for he would continue walking ahead without me. But later, in the store, he said, 'Jo, you seem to know a lot of the townspeople.' I reminded him that I had been born in Utica. 'Oh, yes,' he said, 'I keep forgetting.' How could he forget when we had talked so often of our roots, our love for Upstate New York? That's typical of Edmund: mind intent on the task before him, he had all but forgotten me. I might have been Mrs. Hutchins, his housekeeper, or even Mary Pcolar, his usual chauffeur."

They finally made it to the Boston Store. "I was almost embarrassed when, in that huffing voice of his, he asked someone—no matter that it wasn't a salesperson—where the linen department was. You know, Dick, that I know every counter in that store. It never occurred to him to ask me. He was about to take the stairs when I led him to the elevators. Second floor. I pointed to the pretty colored sheets and the floral ones which were the latest rage. 'Oh, dear me, no, they would give me nightmares.' His instructions to the clerk were for plain white ones; then, turning to me, 'How many should I get?' How to answer that? For *all* the beds? Just his own? I tried quickly to make a mental picture of the beds in that old house. How many were twins? Doubles? 'Why don't you buy two pair for your bed only, and when Elena comes, she'll know better what you need?' That seemed to be the right answer. 'Yes, yes, you're right, Jo.' The clerk, a woman who had waited on me for years, would like to have inquired of me, *who's the queer duck you're with who doesn't know how many sheets he needs?* but asked instead, of Edmund, 'Muslin or percale, all cotton or blends?' 'Wh-wh-what does she mean? Jo, you tell her, you buy what you think is best.' My efforts to explain the differences in quality, feel, price only were making him impatient. The earlier mood was beginning to desert him; he was anxious to get on with his other purchases."

I asked Jo about the footwear he was going to need for his picnic outing.

"In the shoe department, the salesman brought out several pairs of sneakers. He did not know the size of his shoes. 'No, no, no, those are not what I want.' He was becoming cross. 'Those are too heavy to walk in. Don't you have those light-weight ones, tennis shoes?' Had it been anyone but Edmund, I might have been ashamed. 'Tennis shoes?' the salesman queried, clearly put off by this old guy's brusqueness. 'For them you'll have to go to a sporting-goods shop.'"

The lamp department proved an even worse failure. Mrs. Hutchins had written the size on a piece of paper. Jo soon wished she hadn't. "The clerk at whom he thrust the paper was waiting on another customer. 'I want a white silk lampshade *this* size.' 'I'll be with you in a moment, sir.' He rested himself against a counter piled high with marked-down shades; when his arm nudged one, it sent six others toppling. 'Oh, my, my, look what I've done!' He bent down, at great cost, and sought to stand them up again on the counter only to have more tumble. It would have been funny except I was worried. His face was taking on the high color it always does when he gets frustrated or tired. You know the signs, Dick. When the salesgirl could not produce the right size shade and offered one slightly larger, he waved her aside. 'No, no, that won't do,' he fretted, walking away toward the elevators. Descending from the third floor, he asked if we might sit down somewhere. I knew he was not up to going far and suggested the lunch counter, street floor. He beamed. 'Splendid, splendid, and we can have an ice-cream soda. Here, let me carry those sheets.'"

The respite, with ice cream, apparently revived him. But they had not yet made the most vital purchases. The store where he could find everything under one roof had let him down. Jo had a suggestion. Did he feel up to walking across the street to a small shop that carried *only* lamps and shades? "By all means, let's go there." Jo reported success. A clerk produced the right color, right size, but appeared puzzled that the elderly gentleman did not want it wrapped, dismayed that he forgot his change, and, finally, amused to watch him walk out of the store carrying the shade by its center frame.

The four blocks back up Genesee Street must have loomed to Wilson like a climb up Everest. Also aware of this, Jo assumed a mock sternness—the first time ever, with him—and told him he was to wait for her in front of the store. She would pick him up shortly. "Th-th-thank you, Jo. Yes, I'll wuh-wait." Edmund's stutter, which we will always remember poignantly for its signal of initial shyness when we met, now to Jo signified exhaustion.

Minutes later, driving, she asked, "Do you want to go back to the Club—rest up before coming out to the house?" She was mindful of the hour—past three. "But I didn't buy my tennis shoes. One can't go on a picnic without tennis shoes." Didn't he have an old pair of shoes, even slippers? No, long walks in shoes were bad for his gout. It was now obvious that the most important purchase had not been made. She quickly abandoned any idea of trying other shops downtown. Parking was too much of a problem, and he was not up to walking. How about the shopping center in New Hartford, just south of town? Edmund appeared puzzled about its location. "Do you mean those shops one passes on the way to Clinton? The ugly parking lot where that beautiful woods used to be? Do you think we'll be able to buy shoes there?" Jo could see he wanted to go. The drive south on Genesee Street enables one to leave Utica by the most picturesque route. Genesee bisects the city. To the north, one approaches Deerfield Corners and the ascent to the Adirondacks. Going south, as they were that autumn afternoon, a motorist can connect to two of the state's loveliest routes—5, to Syracuse, or, further south, our favorite 20, with rolling hills that are as beautiful as those of my native eastern Pennsylvania—the Poconos.

Going to New Hartford, they passed the now-entering Utica sign that says *Sincerity City*, a kind of anagram for the *Sin City* label that for a time had been attached to Utica after some underworld scandals a decade ago.

"I let him off in front of a Thom McAn store while I parked. Inside, we had to wait our turn. Edmund appeared content to rest in a comfortable chair. I didn't want a repetition of the Boston Store fiasco so I excused myself on some vague pretense to confer with one of the clerks. He did not have tennis shoes—men's, that is. I asked him to bring us a couple of pairs of ladies', sizes 8 and 9. Edmund was delighted. The 9 proved much too large, but he said, 'I'll take them.' I stuck my finger into them behind his heel and pointed out how large they were; that he could well lose them in walking. 'Do you think so, Jo?' Finally with a little persuasion, he settled for the 8. You know, he was totally unaware that he had bought *women's* tennis shoes, that the toes were more pointed than they would be in men's. He was so happy with his purchase that he walked out of the store wearing them."

By now Jo realized it was close on four and time to return to the Club. On the way back Edmund asked if they might make just one more stop. "I really would like to buy some new records to shave to." "For *what?*" She had not understood. "I like to play music when I'm shaving, and all my old records are rather scratchy." She tried to think where the record shops were. She remembered Worden's, near Grant's bookstore, catty-cornered across the street from the Fort Schuyler. That he knew Worden's, and had bought records there before, became quickly apparent. Boyd Golder, the proprietor, addressed him by name. No thumbing through the selections; he knew exactly what he wanted: a Gilbert and Sullivan and a Vivaldi, the exact titles of which Jo had forgotten. She now knew at least two of the places Edmund patronized in Utica.

As they were about to leave, Edmund hesitated. "Jo, I want to buy you something. Pick out a record or two." No, she said, being with him was pleasure enough. Edmund was not to be put off. Would she like one of those pens with plastic flowers on their ends? Then he thought better; they would not suit her: too gaudy. "Ah, I know what I shall buy you." In that way he had, when intent on a single purpose, he marched on ahead to Grant's, a few stores further on.

"Do you have a copy of Peterson's *Field Guide to the Birds?*"

"Oh, we do indeed, Mr. Wilson."

Jo now knew his third shopping place.

"I'll take it. Wrap it nicely . . . uh, with a bow." Turning to Jo, he said, "Peterson's is best for identifying birds. Now you can tell me what appears at *your* feeder. I'm sure you don't get as many birds at your place as I do at mine. A flock of Evening Grosbeaks came through my yard last week. Have you seen any, Jo?" Jo was delighted. "Oh, dear, I should have inscribed it. Remind me to do it at the house."

The Peterson's *Guide* rests on our coffee table in College Station, Texas, a place which is considered a bird watcher's paradise. But the book was never inscribed by its giver. Jo simply forgot to ask.

By now their day surely had to come to a close. They walked slowly to the Club. At the corner, waiting for the light to change, he said, "It's been such a lovely day, hasn't it, Jo? B-b-but would you mind terribly if I didn't come to dinner tonight?"

"You're tired," she said. "Of course I don't mind."

"No it's not that I'm tired. I just think I should not overdo. I want to be in good shape when Elena comes tomorrow. And I ought to check my reading for the symposium."

"I helped him with his three purchases. Without any ceremony he said, 'Goodbye, my dear, and th-th-thank you so much. Don't forget to send me your story.'

"Can you imagine, Dick. It was *not* just the drinks. He really *wants* to read my story."

The thought warmed her all the way home, but it would be several months before she was to bring it to him at Talcottville.

☙ XI ❧

The Farewell Years

*I*N SOME WAYS, the last times I saw Edmund were among the least memorable. Except for chauffeuring him to and from Talcottville several times, I was rarely alone with him. I suspect I was poor company anyway; the post-doctoral doldrums had set in. When finally, in January 1970, I was invited to give a talk on W. Somerset Maugham at Texas A&M University, it was a godsend. The paper led to a job offer. By the time Edmund, despite having suffered a coronary the previous month, made his annual May pilgrimage, Jo and I knew we were bound for Texas.

How could we know we were never to see him again?

I can only present the last two summers in terms of excerpts that are drawn from a dozen letters. After seven years, we expected Edmund's phone call every time he came to Talcottville. If I was not exactly taking Edmund Wilson for granted—had anyone ever done that?—I no longer wished to be a recorder of every word and gesture. The following notes illustrate the shorthand that now characterized my monitorship:

1969

Sunday May 25: Edmund Wilson has been up here two weeks. O'Donnell saw him last week. Reports that he looks somewhat feebler since last summer. He told Tom he would be phoning us soon. The college is probably going to hire Mary Pcolar—in the PR office.

Tuesday June 24: Edmund phoned early Saturday and invited us to join him for dinner Sunday—at the Parquay. He showed us the manuscript of Svetlana Alliluyeva's second book. She had been staying with the Wilsons at Wellfleet. He thinks the new work will be of vast historical importance. The portrait of Stalin is brutal—so brutal that the publisher is afraid of inherent puritanism in American readers that will take form of a detestation of Svetlana for hating her father so. Tom O'Donnell had prepared me for a man who, at seventy-four, had declined the last year. I thought he looked better than last fall. He is without lower teeth while a precision man in Lowville prepares a bridge for him.[1] He is reduced to soups and, yes, Wheatina.

He had just read the Carlos Baker biography of Hemingway.[2] He opposes the position taken by his friend Elizabeth Hardwick in her review in *New York Review of Books*. She said, in effect, that everything worth saying about Hemingway the artist has been said (she praised Philip Young's book[3] and Wilson's essays) and that Baker's minutiae only play into the image of the public Hemingway. Wilson believes otherwise. The Baker digging is important because it casts a brighter light on Hemingway's masochism, his hatreds, and his terrible vindictiveness. Edmund, who says he has contracted malaria from a five-week stay in Jamaica during February and March, tells another Hemingway story picked up on the island from a hotelman—one the man claims Hemingway told him years ago at the Hemingway estate in Cuba. Hemingway, on safari in Africa, caught the scent of a kudu. Papa claimed the kudu knew he was the Great White Hunter and encouraged the pursuit. Finally he saw the kudu by moonlight and had a shot at it. The shot wounded the animal, who escaped while still, according to Papa, knowing and wanting the pursuit. Days later, Hemingway came on the kudu who charged toward him as Hemingway fired. The kudu, Hemingway related in drunken tears, died in his arms. Wilson sees in it further evidence of Hemingway's perverted masculinity.

Wilson orders four small bottles of Rhine wine while eating almost nothing. Back at the house, I presented him a copy of the first issue, under Jo's and my ownership, of *Quartet*. We told him that the little magazine, started in 1961, had gone broke at Purdue and we were taking it over. Jo inadvertently touched a sore spot. We could only make a go of *Quartet* as a team, she explained, with me handling the manuscripts and editorial end and she the books and subscriptions. Didn't he think it was lucky when a couple shared similar interests? There was a pause. "It wuh-wuh- it was— hideous!" he exclaimed, and we knew.

In today's mail, a check from Edmund Wilson for three years of *Quartet*. I doubt if I shall cash it. Great, great old guy.

5 July (my 48th birthday): Edmund phoned. Will have dinner with us Friday. Asked me to bring up the Wiener transla- tions of Tolstoy's plays. Did I know the translator was the father of Norbert?

31 July: Edmund is not sure it was malaria he picked up in Jamaica. Plans to go to a hospital in Boston where he says they know more about tropical diseases than in northern New York. He says Rosalind, his older daughter, is occupying the old house. She does not, he says, enjoy meeting his Utica friends. The same goes for Elena, apparently, although she was lovely and charming the two occasions we met her. We are not among those who are asked up there when Elena is with him.

Austin Briggs, a young teacher of American Literature at Hamilton College, has a book coming out on Harold Frederic from Cornell University Press, and Edmund tells me he has asked *The New Yorker* to release his long overdue essay so as to catch the publication date of the Briggs volume. His article will also plug Tom O'Donnell's book[4] on Frederic.

Monday, 22 September: I have been reading the current *Atlantic* for Wilson's memoir of Edwin O'Connor and their col- laboration. Enjoyed the memoir but soon gave up on the latter. The surprise in the memoir was a reference to Edmund and friends on the beach. I don't think of Edmund as lolling on the beach. Once, though, he told me that he enjoyed the swimming at Well- fleet and regretted almost more than any other restriction of his angina that he can no longer go swimming.

Tuesday, 14 October: Jo is having dinner tonight with Edmund. They will probably see "Medium Cool." I teach a class tonight.

Thursday, 23 October: Edmund came to dinner. He sat for

some minutes with all of us, Phil included, teaching us a fascinating but complicated game of double solitaire. He made a standing offer that any of us could send a collect telegram any time we "beat" the game. I played more than a hundred times over the next few days, came near winning only twice. Philip and Jo had no near wins at all. I played chauffeur Sunday—Talcottville to Utica and back. Going back got us into the heaviest fog I can recall in Deerfield Hill (around 9 P.M.). Recalling our first drive, when he sat riveted in his seat, I found this time *he* actually relaxed *me*. We talked about teaching and how generally unrewarding it is. "Do you think it's the getting-on-to-fifty business?" I asked. "A man has two bad times," Edmund said. "When he passes 30 and when he reaches 50. If he makes it safely to 50, he can make it the rest of the way." I told him I was seeing a psychiatrist for depression. "I think you'd be better off if you were writing more," he said.

1970

Sunday, 12 April: Edmund is in Cape Cod Hospital, Hyannis, after a heart attack. I learned through one of my students, Gretchen Crosten of Boonville, a friend of Wilson's and of Rosalind Wilson's.[5] Jo wrote him a long letter. My friend Earle Birney was here for a reading at Utica College. He is incontestably the best *reader* I have ever heard. And a superb raconteur. He had somehow thought Edmund Wilson would be present for the party afterward at our house. I brought Charles Helmsing, who is also Canadian and from the West, to meet Earle, who piped up with, "How do you do, Mr. Wilson, I've been anxious to meet you for a long time."[6] The evening survived that embarrassing start. Earle, who is 65 and more like a taller Walt Whitman every time I see him, was in superb form.

Wednesday, 3 June: Edmund phoned Sunday and we joined him for a drink at the Diplomat in North Utica (he calls it the Diplomatic). He wanted to go to the Fort Schuyler, but it is closed Sundays. He couldn't have been in better spirits. With him was Mary Pcolar—the first time I'd seen them together since the *were-you-ever-a-Communist?* thing in my class almost six years ago. Edmund is sponsoring a trip for Mary and her teen-age daughter to Hungary this summer. At least I gathered that he was footing the bill—a gesture, he implied, whose purpose was to learn what Mary, a first generation Hungarian-American, thinks of present-day Hungary. I couldn't help but notice—and Jo, a severe critic of her sex, agrees—how pretty Mary looked.

Edmund allows Mary to take him to what he calls "Utica's porn films." He had just seen one called "Without a Stitch" ("awful!") and, earlier, "The Grasshopper" ("worth seeing," although he never made it clear why). Jo and I asked him if he had seen the Ken Russell version of *Women in Love*. He had and thought it all rather silly ("two grown men fighting with their penises flopping about"). He has never read the novel either. "D. H. Lawrence was a hysterical fellow, and I have never cared much for his books. I saw him in person only once. It was at a publisher's party in London in his honor. He began ranting about the universe, how futile civilized living was, including publisher's parties. He could never live down his appearance. A little like Wells in that. Lawrence had an inordinantly small head. He never got over feeling inferior among the upper-crust English with whom he was always thrown in. He had Midlands coal miner written in every feature."

Edmund consumed three martinis, and I two. It was only when we rose, with him building himself to his feet, that I could see how feeble physically he has become in the years I've known him. Each step is a risk. As we watched him struggle into Mary's car, it was obvious how much his last heart attack has taken out of him.

Thursday, 11 June: Edmund phoned yesterday and we will be having dinner and seeing a film together tonight.

Edmund continues to allow himself to be taken to the stag films that are trying to pass for commercial cinema here. I believe that, reduced as he is to a completely sedentary existence, he finds relaxation in watching porn films. We three will see "The Visit," with Ingrid Bergman and Anthony Quinn. The film had no sooner begun than Edmund complained of feeling ill. We took him back to the Fort Schuyler where he spent the night.

I recall that the late Westbrook Pegler was supposed to have said the only worthwhile event in his adult life was Disney's "Snow White and the Seven Dwarfs." If one were to seek a similar cinematic milestone of Wilson's old age, it would be the Beatles and "The Yellow Submarine." He keeps telling us to be sure and see it when it comes around again and especially be on the lookout for an engaging "egghead" named Jeremy, for people called the Blue Meanies, and for a song titled "The Nowhere Man." Edmund still remembers snatches of the lyrics.

Jo just answered the phone. Edmund wants to make sure I'll be driving him back tonight. Also, could Jo pick up for him another pair of sneakers like the ones they bought together a while back? Jo and I conjecture who will be picnicking with him along the Sugar River. Can the man who looked so feeble go hiking?

Later Charles Helmsing called. He's like a character out of Restoration drama—with an accent. Has been manager of the Fort Schuyler a little over a year and already he knows dark secrets of many of Utica's Four Hundred. He tells us that Edmund came in last week with Many Pcolar. He and Charles began discussing Oscar Wilde. According to Charles, Mary thought they were talking about *Cornell* Wilde whom Wilson had never heard of. As Helmsing tells it, the three-way conversation never got back on the track.

Thursday, 18 June: Edmund tells us that he is finding evenings alone at the old house increasingly difficult to endure. "One marries so as to have someone to laugh with at night," he observed last Sunday. But Elena leads so full a social life at Wellfleet that she invariably declines to come up to the country with him. She also has had an auto accident recently, and Edmund fears to have her drive up here. "All the young women I love are married." He repeats a refrain that Jo has heard before but of which she never tires. This time he adds a note. "Elena resents any reference I make to other women, especially attractive ones," he tells us. Edmund referred to Jo, to Mary, and to a third "girlfriend" whom he has not identified.

Last Wednesday we took him to the New Hartford shopping center for a second pair of sneakers. He'd made a date with his third girlfriend to explore Sugar River below the old railroad bridge, where there is a swimming hole and cataract. Jo unearthed from the shoe stacks a pair of the lady's sneakers she remembered from the previous expedition. Edmund liked them immediately. That they were women's made no difference before and none now.

On Sunday Edmund phoned. Mabel Hutchins would bring him to Utica, where he had arranged to meet Phito and Eva Thoby-Marcelin. Could the five of us have a reunion at our house? Phito's new novel, *All Men Are Mad* (translated from the French by Eva), had got a good review in *Newsweek*, and Edmund's introduction was appearing in *The New York Review of Books*. Wilson had been absolutely indefatigable in Phito's behalf just as Malcolm Lowry had been earlier. Edmund calls the book Phito's "masterpiece." I have now read it. It reminds me of Guareschi's *Little World of Don Camillo*. The humor is at a distance from urban American jadedness, and I did not find the novel as readable as Edmund did. (*Inserted digression*: Lately Jo and I have spent several weeks on St. Kitts, West Indies, where Philip was, at time of writing, a Peace Corps volunteer, teaching science and math in Cayon, a village of 600. Everyone knows everyone else. There are no secrets, little crime. I thought of Phito's novel and determined to go back to it.)

He acknowledges my Joyce, Aiken, Lowry essay in *University of Toronto Quarterly* and one titled "Malcolm Lowry and the Addictions of an Era," which had just appeared in the *University of Windsor Review*.[7] "You appear to be having luck in Canadian journals." He said nothing that would indicate he had finished either article. "All that cabbala stuff and occultism bore me," he said, producing that high-pitched staccato delivery that he takes on whenever issuing a judgment. "I'm afraid nothing could induce me to read *Under the Volcano*. Too late." He did have one comment on my "addictions" piece. Either I or the printer had the accent mark going the wrong way in *terribilità*.

Entering his seventy-sixth year, Edmund told us that he tries for six pages of first-draft every morning and then devotes what's left of his working day to polishing those six. He is finding his current work hard going. It is to be a book on his northern New York forbears and himself, including the history of the old stone house. "Such dull stuff—extremely hard to be scholarly where I have so many peoples' versions of everything." He feels he has a chance of finishing the book this summer. Much will be drawn from entries in the diaries he has kept since 1951, when his mother died and he began coming up here.

On Edmund's insistence, the five of us—Edmund, Eva and

Phito, Jo and I—drove to the Austin Briggses, a couple made for Hamilton College, where a professor's social poise is as important as his scholarship. Austin was at his lilacs when we arrived—a redhead of perhaps thirty (I learned later that he had just turned thirty-nine), casual, attractive. His wife Margaret is a Southern belle. I thought she seemed nervous—as who wouldn't be? Five guests, including Edmund Wilson, just dropping by! Wilson warmed her up by asking her to tell her Ezra Pound story—one he had told before. The Briggses were the official hosts a year ago to the octogenarian poet, who was to receive another honorary degree from his alma mater. Pound had in late years adopted a silence that was as legendary as the loquacity of his earlier persona. When Margaret asked whether he would have light meat or dark, he answered, "Just as it comes." As he departed he made an unintelligible apology for giving Margaret so much trouble. He was gowned for the ceremony, still, in Margaret's view, handsome, and he received a tremendous ovation.

Later, at our house, Edmund says it has been his fate to meet many great writers early in their careers and only once. I wanted to say it has been mine to meet many *late* and only once—Maugham, Aiken, others. We talked about E. M. Forster, who had just died at ninety. "I met him at a London literary cocktail party at a time when I was considerably more to the left. I was introduced to Forster, whose books I have never much cared for, and I told him that I agreed with his high opinion of *War and Peace* and the works of Balzac but that I thought *Das Kapital* belonged in the same empyrean. Forster demurred, started to say something like 'But *Das Kapital* is not—.' I never heard the rest of his remark because somebody came between us. We never got back to our chat."

I said I also felt indebted to Forster who, along with Kenneth Rexroth, was just about the only major artist who favored Wells in his controversy with Henry James.[8] "Favoring Wells in that instance is not hard to do," said Edmund. "But few do," I replied. We had been over that ground. Edmund thinks James, the great writer, should have won out over James, the great artist. James ought, he believes, to have answered Wells in kind rather than merely writing the sort of letter—powerful though the letter was—that Wells could not possibly understand.

He tells us he is seriously trying to sell the old house and even called on people from the New York State Historical Association at Cooperstown. The place costs double to heat what the place in Wellfleet costs. The plumbing doesn't work.

He is going back to Wellfleet on June 23, unusual for him, and doesn't expect to return until mid-August. He tells us he wants to be sure to see us before we leave for Texas. Son Reuel and his wife and the grandson have come in from the West Coast for his new job at Western Ontario University, London, Ontario, Canada. There appears to be something amiss between him and Rosalind, who he says has moved out of the old house. We still have never met her. All Edmund will say is that the old house is too much for her. In a comment to Charles Helmsing, Edmund makes, for only the second time—and first time, directly—a reference to Mary McCarthy. Charles, who is something of a predator for gossip, asked him, although he must have known, if he had been married to M. M. "For seven years," Edmund answered. "She remarried and lives in Paris."

Jo and he talk with verve about houses, flowers, wild-growing things. My ears prick up. Jo mentioned and described an unusual butterfly she had seen on the car visor. "Are you sure it wasn't a moth?" Wilson asked. "When Nabokov was at Cornell I used to phone him from Talcottville whenever I saw something I thought might interest a lepidopterist. He knew the Latin and everything conceivable about any species I'd mention."

Yesterday, while I was teaching, Jo, Edmund, and Charles went to the Sadaquada, an upper-crust private golf club near Clinton. Jo later reported the afternoon warm and easy. It was on this occasion that Edmund repeated the remark about all the women he loves being married.

Jo and Edmund, at his request, stopped for records. Despite his admiration for "The Yellow Submarine," he did not buy the new Beatles album. Instead, a Berlioz, a Ravel (he adores *Bolero*), and something by the Boston Pops.

4th of July: A letter from Edmund. I had written him that my final course at Utica College is one on the Continental novel. He shocks me by saying he has never read *Don Quixote*. What astounds is not so much that he has missed a classic but that he freely admits to missing it. Another kind of noblesse oblige perhaps. Wilson's Hispanophobia is well known. He repeats too freely for anyone to miss it that Spain has contributed little. Even Picasso falls short. For Edmund, Picasso, while intent on shocking, never omits something the ordinary person can recognize. His behavior and his art are equally vulgar.

Monday, 17 August: Edmund returned from Wellfleet yesterday. It appears we will see him once more before our departure for Texas in eight days. Jo phoned him this afternoon. We have a date for Sunday, at the old house.

I have no letter covering that last Sunday, late August 1970. Neither Edmund nor we thought it would be the last time. The talk was mostly of houses. Edmund expressed pleasure that we planned to keep ours in Utica. The last words of his that I remember were about why he keeps up his house at enormous expense. He enjoyed "galvanizing" the old house into life, making it express his own personality and interests, filling it with his own imagination, feeling a continuity with everybody who has lived there, basing himself on them. These were not the words, but they paraphrase the sentiment I remember.

"I feel more comfortable in this old house than anywhere else in the world." This he *did* say. And yet, during that last conversation, he spoke of selling the old place. We hoped not.

However, the final chapter of his last book published during his lifetime, at the end of *Upstate*, he dismissed the possibility. Although he would prefer to be lord of a manor, no highways for miles, he vowed to keep up the old house. He had resigned himself to go on living. At sixty, Wilson denied that he existed in a pocket of the past. "I may find myself here at the center of things," he wrote in *A Piece of My Mind*,[9] "since the center can be only in one's head." A month after his seventieth birthday, he wrote of a nightmare in which he was dispossessed of his house but follows with two joyful pages on the discovery near his property of the showy Ladyslipper. Finally, approaching eighty and with "old fogeyism comfortably setting in," he took stock at the end of *Upstate*. The knowledge that death might not be far away made earthly affairs unimportant and human beings barbarous. Yet, in his first letter which crossed mine after our move to Texas, he writes about his twenty-fifth book, an updating of his classic study of the rise of socialism, *To the Finland Station*.

The Seignorial Stance

W E NEVER SAW HIM begin to die. The move to Texas spared us that. If whatever physical zest he showed had something of the nervous perkiness of old age, his color had always been good, his spirits, after settlement of his income taxes, amiable, his attention ever forward: the next day, the next book.

Then the letters, as faithful as ever, began to show disquieting signs. I wrote him in the middle of our first winter away to inquire if a Texas-size honorarium might induce him south out of the New England arctic. If I knew his answer, I was unprepared for its tone.

"Dear Costas," he began, 9 March 1971, *"Fortuna molto mi dispiace adesso* [I much dislike my life these days]. I'm glad to hear that you're liking Texas, but should hate to have you sell your Utica house. Though physically somewhat shaken, I expect to get back to Talcottville in May—if only to see what is happening about the road in front of my house."

I was not to learn until my return, two years after his death, that he had been fighting New York State's attempts to eliminate certain approaches to his beloved Sugar River. To do so entailed building an elevated widened span across the waters and taking a large piece of Wilson's front lawn for the bridge's southern approach. Two lanes would become four. Edmund lost. You could tell in a minute, just by looking, how much closer the highway came to his front door.

His letter was longer than usual, a catalog of complaints. *Upstate* would be out from Farrar, Straus & Giroux late that summer of 1971. We should not read the parts that were about to run serially in *The New Yorker*. "They have left out the historical and family chapters and omitted the most interesting episodes from the diary—so that it reads like *Walden, or Life in the Woods*—all about the birds and flowers . . . and this leaves me practically a hermit." One cheerful allusion leaked in. He had finally completed reading *Middlemarch*, which in turn completed a cycle of reference in our friendship. He had told me years ago that when he was living in the old house he could imagine himself in a George Eliot novel, seignorial, lord of the manor.

Coming to Texas, though, was out. Didn't I remember he could not lecture; only read things he had written—like the Little Water Ceremony of the Iroquois?

Then we did not hear from him for three and a half months. June, a month when his presence in Talcottville could be depended upon, brought a typewritten note—but from Wellfleet. He had suffered a fall, "hurt my back badly and am now more or less of a cripple." Still, he was hopeful of a reunion with Jo, who with Philip would be spending three months of the summer Upstate mainly to see (for the last time, as it turned out) her eighty-year-old father, and to sell some of the furniture we had left behind. From Utica she wrote me of getting no answer at the old house. Later, in a letter, Jo learned that Edmund had phoned, too—but in September. She had returned to Texas in August.

Christmas brought no cheer. Instead of one of his extraordinary cards that were really little books, he sent us a note saying that he was not sending any that year. I wonder if there had ever been another cardless Christmas for Edmund Wilson. "Holiday Greetings from Edmund Wilson" was not a card; it was a liberal education, a new edition of an old Wilson, shy erotica. There were limericks (not up to Conrad Aiken's standards but illustrated by his own cartoons: *A Young millionairess named Laura/ Had a passion for fauna and flora./ She installed a large zoo/ And an orchid house, too,/ and maintained a superb manticora*); "fabulous word squares," in which four mini-crossword puzzles, five letters down, five across, could be built from rhyming-couplet questions, part lore, part gag; multi-lingual *jeux d'esprit* ("something for my Italian friends," "something for my Hungarian friends"); something for everybody.

After Christmas the Wilsons did go south—but to Florida, two months. Writing on January 27, 1972 from Naples on the Gulf Coast, he was finding life "duller than anything you can imagine, but I am somewhat better." He must have been. The man whom Dwight Macdonald found "always on duty" was. He was writing a preface for a new edition of *To the Finland Station,* collecting what would be his last book of essays, and had put together his studies of Russian writers from Gogol to Solzhenitsyn. This making of new books from old was indeed his salvation.

Two months later, the Wilsons were back in Wellfleet. In the next-to-last letter he ever wrote me (March 28, 1972), Edmund thanked me for an eight-page review-memoir in *Quartet* on the occasion of the appearance of *Upstate.* He made five corrections, all in the memoir portion:

—The Talcottville place was maternal not paternal.

—"My nose is not turned up: it is perfectly straight."

—"The trick you speak of is done not by flicking the card: the card turns over by itself."

—Ezra Pound did make one other remark at lunch. When asked what his impressions were on revisiting New York City, he said, "Too many people."

—"The old Post Office was not, as you say, in a desk of the old house but is now used as a china closet."

The final letter I ever received from him was dated May 15, 1972, a week after his seventy-seventh birthday. I noted it earlier, but it bears repeating here:

> Dear Dick and Jo:
>
> I have had a slight stroke and can't talk properly, but I hope to get up to Talcottville for the latter part of May and June. . . . I don't know what the Italians call those photographers. [1]
>
> Best wishes,
>
> Edmund W

He had less than four weeks to live when he wrote that letter. At mid-morning of Monday, June 12, I received a phone call in my office from Charles Helmsing. Edmund had died early that morning in the old house. Charles was concerned that we not hear it first on the TV news or read it in the newspaper. He thought Jo and I would be comforted to know Edmund had apparently died in his sleep.[2]

Later on the same day, Charles phoned again. He had seen Wilson at the Fort Schuyler as recently as the previous Thursday. With him for dinner was the young and attractive wife of his dentist, Anne Miller, still another, as he always put it, of "my favorite women, all of whom are married to somebody else." Charles, who had not seen him since the previous September, was shocked at how much ground he had lost. Leaning on his walking-stick and supported by Anne Miller, Edmund looked gray, cadaverous. Somehow his escort piloted him across Genesee Street to the Stanley Theater to see *The French Connection*.

Of the funeral, whether it would be in Talcottville or Wellfleet, Helmsing knew nothing. As it turned out, there was a simple service, his body lying in state on his old brass bed that had been moved to the first floor, followed by cremation, and a memorial service two days later at Wellfleet. Separated as I was by some sixteen hundred miles, I knew none of these things. A fuller report of my interview with Mary Pcolar two years later is in Chapter 16.

During the long first day of our grief, we heard his passing accorded less than a 30-second "spot" and second billing on the Cronkite news to the passing of a minor labor leader.

No large questions occurred to us. We remembered the way he always greeted us at the door. "Huh-huh-how are you two?" Then he would smile, though his bridgework narrowed that smile, and you would see the sparkle in the eyes, the openness of his happiness at seeing us again. "Wuh-wuh-won't you come in?" We did not know it until we knew each other well enough never to think about it: the stutter was his ice-breaker. *We* were not always on time, but *he* was always on time. If we were to go to dinner, there would never be any hurry. He would have us sit in the old rockers while he puttered toward the kitchen for the pint of Johnny Walker, the glasses, the ice. At first, though we now barely remembered, he had had soda in a squirt bottle, the only time I ever saw one except in old films; but when it worked less and less well, he discarded it. The good talk, the double-take, the back-track ("trashy, really!"), the reassessment, always unguarded (except for Anthony West), the scandalous anecdote ("You must promise to stop me if you've heard . . ."), the huffing and puffing, no houses blown down. The laughter.

I thought of his last polemic—against the widening of the highway in front of his house, cutting down the old elm tree to do it. I remembered an old woman, Caroline Bullock—about Wilson's age, too—whose plight I had written up once. Not only her front lawn but her whole house was knocked off by an arterial. Caroline simply accepted it that a man-made marvel like a super highway could swallow up her property. She took the state's pittance and moved.

Yet Edmund Wilson went to the courts over six feet of "encroachment." For him, in his season Upstate, only the local young men on their motorcycles, or drag-racers, used the road, making those sputtering noises that disturbed his squirearchical calm. He was never there winters when the skiers from Utica and points south made good use of the extra lane—a wider and safer ribbon of ice—on the only direct route to the slopes of Turin.

Wasn't this, like the income-tax business, unworthy of the author of *Patriotic Gore*?

The highway and Sugar River and his front lawn are simply not the point. Authenticity is. The "unreconstructed isolationist"— Mary McCarthy's term for him during a larger war—refused to the end to be a retread to progress. In a world that in his view was being run by engineers, bureaucrats, and the armed forces, he would be a nationalistic movement of one against the elimination of benevolent noblesse oblige, his article of faith for the way he wrote and the way he lived. Maybe that was what our neighbor from Talcottville meant with his courtliness that was really concern.

PART TWO

Afterwords

Summer 1974

In his self-interview, published when he was nearing seventy, Edmund Wilson reflected with teasing irony his sense that he was not alive at all. He admitted to not knowing what was happening in his own country—or caring—and of finding that the London he once knew wasn't there any more. As the interview closed, Wilson "floats up to his study," resolved to make an effort not to evaporate.

Now he had truly left us. Eulogies appeared everywhere—Roger Straus in the daily, Wilfrid Sheed in the Sunday *New York Times*; Cyril Connolly in the *Sunday Times* of London, and Philip Toynbee in *The Observer*.[1] Some, like Harry Levin and Frederick Exley, delayed their tributes more than two years and wrote monographs.[2] Between the immediate responses and the delayed ones came my favorite—by Barry Callaghan, the son of Edmund's old friend. His relationship was like mine; namely, that of a close-but-not-intimate friend who for a short time felt himself charged by a vital energy source. "Though we may want to weep that he is dead, his triumph makes a man just a little ashamed at how little he has done; yet, at the same time, we are encouraged by what he achieved to go on and do more, to be true to our own best talents: obstinately, with as much grace as possible, with all energy. That is how Edmund lives with me now."[3]

Still later, I read how another friend[4] found in Edmund's *Night Thoughts* these words that seem almost to be issuing, cheerfully, from the grave:

> So these the precepts are, my friends,
> The aging Wilson recommends:
>
> Beware of dogmas backed by faith;
> Steer clear of conflicts to the death;
>
> Keep going; never stoop; sit tight;
> Read something luminous at night.
>
> And if no ready means you find
> To cultivate this state of mind,
>
> Why, you must come to see me here
> —If not next year, another year.[5]

Double Meanings

New lines are wreathed on old lines half erased,
And those on older still: and so forever,
The old shines through the new and colors it.
What's new? What's old? All things have double meanings.
— Conrad Aiken "Palimpsest"

*I*T IS LATE AFTERNOON of one of those days in the Upstate
summer that make anywhere else at this season diminished. I sit in
my car with the Texas plates. From my vantage on Main Street in
Boonville, time and place play games with memory.

Below me, around the block from Kramer's Pharmacy,
Main winds south through the village to Route 12, which circles
Boonville like a belt. It ascends north to the Adirondacks or de-
scends south to the foothills and Utica. A construction gang works
fretfully here in the middle of the village at some new widening of
this feeder to 12. I see that I shall not be able to reach the highway
in the way I remember; traffic is being rerouted around the huge
scar in Main Street. It was the same four years ago, the last time I
was here, when I said goodbye to my friend, Edmund Wilson. I
think of him now, expressing pleasure in that way he had of bringing his hand to cultivate the thinnest of patches at the back of his
head. That last time he expressed pleasure when we told him that,
although we were moving to Texas, we planned to keep our house
in Utica. "It's Jo's idea, I have no roots," I said to one who never for
a moment forgot his. "That's a pity," he replied, responding to me
but glancing at Jo.

I think of him now and how seignorial he was, his Marxist
phase notwithstanding; how little he was disposed to accept any
notion that in the country he once loved individual good had to

give way to the collective benefit. Half a continent away the last three summers, I had to follow by the inferences of his brief letters not only his battles against strokes, angina, the gout but also his maverick and losing battle with the State of New York to protect that tiny patch of his seignory—his front lawn—from the bulldozers. Earlier today I saw the evidence of Wilson's defeat: the white cement curb which brought the kind of commerce he hated six feet closer to his door. I think, too, as I prepare to drive back down Deerfield Hill to Utica, how fitting it was that he never learned to operate a car. Even if there was a factor of manual dexterity involved, as his cousin Otis Munn insisted to me—even if Cousin Edmund *was* mechanically infirm—how authentic a gesture for one who rebelled against the conversion of the nation into a complex of white-striped veins connected to four-lane arteries.

Above me, looking toward the innards of the village behind the mall and bandstand, I see markers pointing in three directions. They jog memory. Alternate Route 12D goes north—to Lowville, where Edmund found, at last, the right dentist. For the driver not intent on exceeding the speed limit to reach resorts like Alexandria Bay and the Thousand Islands, 12D is the only way, less than three miles, to the limestone house around which Edmund Wilson created a small and benevolent—unbelievably benevolent—squirearchy. For eight summers, the old stone house was one of the points of triangulation without which it was impossible to locate myself in the world to which I, an outsider, sought entry.

I was not the only outsider. Another marker—no route number this time—notes *West Leyden 3 miles*. Still a country road, it is only lately having the "country" taken out of it by asphalt. If I took the West Leyden cutoff for just over three miles I would pass the farmhouse where Mary Horbach Pcolar lives: Edmund's esteemed *Mariska*. To her, he was, in person, always *Mr. Wilson* or, in letters, *Kedves Odon Basci (My Dear Uncle Edmund).*[1] For twelve summers, the old house was also for her a point of triangulation, and the death two years before of its seasonal occupant left her, for a time, a woman without direction.

Something of the story of these two has been vividly reported by Frederick Exley in *Pages from a Cold Island*,[2] a book whose elegiac celebration of Wilson often strains against the autobiographical excesses of the rest of the book. Exley refers to Mary

Pcolar as Wilson's "last passion" but is careful to protect his meaning by presenting the words within quotation marks. A passion of his she certainly was, although probably not in the usual way; their relationship was vital to those of his last years that were spent Upstate. For wasn't Edmund always, in letters and diaries alike, apologizing for an inability to do "justice" to his relationship with Mary Pcolar? Although she may have read none of his books but *Upstate* through and was unlikely to have discussed anyone else's either, who in the country of his summers could claim more of him?

For a moment, I turn to *Upstate*. It rests, the last of his books to be published during his lifetime, on the car seat beside me, blue-covered, sized like all of his books to fit into a man's coat pocket. Somewhere between the entries—two decades' worth of diaries—that contain the names of every person, famous and unknown alike, who ever visited the old house; somewhere, not quite drowned in the genealogical deluge, may lie *the* secret of the vitality that continued almost to the end.

For the reader gratefully accustomed to expect of any subject Edmund Wilson tackled, however complex, a distillation, the reading of *Upstate* must be something of a chore. For the Wilsonian, what charges the book is a current of irony that the man who had been perhaps America's most truthful intellectual chronicler between the wars no longer felt at home anywhere but at one rural outpost of it. What makes the book the most autobiographically revealing of his nonfiction is what it tells of the failure of noblesse oblige for a mandarin who saw that even the perquisites of privilege—privacy, continuity, relevance—were disappearing. And what gives *Upstate* major intrinsic interest is its suggestion of a wound-and-bow synthesis in the life of the man who made the phrase famous.

It grows late in the day, as I thumb the pages, and I want to avoid the twilight when the long descent down Deerfield Hill to Utica can be treacherous. I look, finally, at the title page where he always, in that fine hand of his and closing with *coll' affezione sincera*, penned an inscription. But just this once there was none. Edmund was dying, and he knew it, when the book appeared in 1971. It came to Jo and me in Texas, impersonally, courtesy of Farrar, Straus & Giroux.

What follows is a kind of updating of the past, backdating of the present. Memory does that. As in the Aiken poem, it becomes an overlay, a varnish, on the actual past, like parchment from which writing has been partially erased to make room for another text. Memory works finally as decoder, probing flux, relentlessly selecting.

❦ XIV ❧

Writers and Neighbors: Walter D. Edmonds

A T WELLFLEET, Edmund Wilson was a writer among writers. Upstate, the literary situation was quite different. He could phone neighbors on Cape Cod like Edmund O'Connor, Arthur Schlesinger, Wilfrid Sheed, Conrad Aiken, just to mention the names he mentioned in my presence. At Talcottville he had Walter D. Edmonds.

To Upstaters, the name Walter D. Edmonds is much more a household one than Wilson's. The titles of his early novels have the right sound—*Rome Haul, Drums Along the Mohawk*. Although Edmonds like Wilson preferred not to brave the Upstate winters—he lives most of the year at Concord, Massachusetts—most Upstaters considered him one of them more than they did the world figure who, as a mostly absentee owner, kept up the old stone house he had inherited at his mother's death when he was already fifty-six.

I met Edmonds through Wilson in August 1963, but when, eleven years later, I spent a July morning with him on his rural estate in Boonville, called Northlands, neither of us remembered the meeting.

I found a reference to it buried among my notes on the third, the briefest, of the conversations with Edmund that first summer. I start with it now only because of remarks the older writer made. They and Edmonds' gentle and humane rebuttals, I believe, isolate certain truths about the possibilities of close kinship among professionals who have in common only the happenstance of a salutary geography and the fact that each applies pen to paper for his living.

"I like Edmonds immensely, but I can't read his novels," Wilson had said. I do not believe he intended to write Edmonds off so easily. One cannot read his collected letters without recognizing his desire to see those friends of his who were also writers make good so that he might do literary journalism about them. I sensed a genuine regret that, for him, the writings of his neighbor never provided him such opportunity.

I saw Edmonds for the second time five summers later in 1968. Again a case—but a wrong one, I believe—could be made for believing Wilson's attitude condescending. Chapter X describes how Edmonds and his wife passed our table at the Parquay while Wilson was holding forth deferentially on Edmonds' historical work, *The Musket and the Cross*, which he was certain would be unmercifully flayed by the critics. None of us thought Wilson's comments had been overheard.

But they had—by Edmonds. This I learned at the end of the summer of 1974 when I began the research for this memoir. Walter D. Edmonds invited me to drop in for a chat at his country estate in Boonville.

Northlands is not easy to find, and I would have had my usual problems—I have no sense of direction—had not Mary Pcolar driven me by the Edmonds postal box the day before. Although he lives in Boonville, it is the *village* of Boonville you go through to reach Northlands (Route 12B, the "upper road," as Mary refers to it). A rural, barely improved way, called the Hawkinsville Road, is a left turn out of the village. One drives through heavily forested side roads, near one portion of Edmund's beloved Sugar River. There's another part of it just below the old stone house. One sees waterfalls and limestone: the same limestone from which Wilson's house was built at the end of the eighteenth century.

The tipoff to Walter Edmonds' Northlands is a large red rural mailbox. At that point one turns left, past a sign that urges *drive slowly, children*. The main house—for there is a complex of houses—is clapboarded and rambling. A driveway leads to a fence, beyond which there appear to be cornfields. I park and walk to the front door. "I'm Kay Edmonds," says a trimly attractive woman at the door. "Where is Mrs. Costa?" I explain that Jo is resting up for our upcoming trip back to Texas. Kay Edmonds says she will summon her husband. He appears, a tall, slender man in logger's jacket and work trousers. A stocky terrier, another pyknik like Wilson, Wells, Lowry—Costa, too—keeps vying for my attention, and I am glad to give it. "It's a Jack Russell terrier," Edmonds reports after introductions. "Name's Erlo, which I thought was original but isn't. Comes from something in Upstate lore. These Jack Russells were bred in England; they burrow into the ground and flush out quarry who are then *broken* by the other hounds. Awful idea."

I follow as Edmonds walks up two steps to what proves to be his study. I ask him to account for "that wonderful sound," and he beckons me to the window. I walk to a far window beyond his writing desk and look out on a brook where water flows over rocks. "We've had trout out there all summer." I believe I shall always think of that view from his writing table as what writers talk about—dilettantes especially—when they talk about the ideal atmosphere.

Edmonds begins talking about the announced topic without any preliminaries. "The first time I met Edmund Wilson was while my first wife Eleanor was still alive—she died in 1956. At any rate, I had just recovered from pneumonia. Only two days out of bed. He phoned and asked if someone could pick him up. It was tea-time when we came back here, but I never knew Edmund to drink tea. I knew he liked to drink. I broke out a 1914 bourbon that the Canadian Liquor Commission had bought from British sellers who had obtained the bourbon from us during Prohibition. It had been made into a blend and was called *Ten American Bourbons*. I served him some of that bourbon. Although he was appreciative—he damned well ought to have been—I could see Edmund's nose twitching toward some brownies. I offered him some. He ate brownies and drank bourbon all afternoon.

"Doc Bob Smith tells one about him that tops that combination. One time he was driving past the old house. Thought he'd check on Edmund's health. He found him dining on cold Boston baked beans and champagne. With a mixture like that, I could imagine him floating right out over the Sugar River."

Edmonds finds a way to divert to animals, an adored subject of his. The point of departure is Wilson's acknowledgment that at least the animals in Edmonds' books are well portrayed. Edmonds is convinced that animals possess reasoning powers. He tells of once being beset by a pair of marsh sparrows. They circled above him, close around his head, clearly leading him somewhere. Following those birds, he came to a nest. A little bird was hanging, his foot caught in the cleft of an alder branch. "When I took the creature in my hand there was not a sound. Those birds must have viewed me as their last possible resource. Once I saw two hunting dogs supporting a collie that had been shot by hunters— literally carrying the collie to safety."

We talk of Wilson's voice. For Edmonds, it had a "kind of huffing quality, like the huffing of a snail in danger. But he was a curiously gentle man."

Except, I hasten to add, about books he didn't like. I remind of Wilson's un-gentle attitude about anything by Maugham and my discovery that he had read none of W.S.M.'s best books. Edmonds breaks open a subject he may have been thinking about from the moment he invited me. "The book of mine he was knocking that day at the Parquay was *The Musket and the Cross*. It came out in 1967 and broke a twelve-year writer's block. I don't believe he liked my writing about Indians. Much as I admired *Apologies to the Iroquois* and told him so, he didn't like me telling him, for example, that Indians are diabetic, a further reason for condemning whites for introducing them to alcohol. I don't think he was especially congenial either to my plans to write a book like *Upstate* about *my* origins.

"He came here often, but there was only one unpleasantness in all the years. My son Peter met him. Peter was just back from a year in Iran. He had become firmly pro-Arab. Edmund was just back from Jerusalem. The Gaza Strip materialized on our front porch."

Edmonds' favorite of the books is *To the Finland Station*. I tell him how much *Axel's Castle* helped me in graduate school. Edmonds has not read it. We speak of *Memoirs of Hecate County* and especially the first segment. I shy away from saying "first story" in deference to Wilson's fierce rebuttal at any suggestion that the book was a collection of short stories rather than a novel. We agree

"The Man Who Shot Snapping Turtles" is unforgettable. Edmonds admires *Patriotic Gore*. He's something of a Civil War buff who has always wanted to do a novel about that period. "All but the Introduction. I wrote Edmund about that Introduction, told him he was *loopy*, and years later he admitted to me he had come to know better."[1]

The question of how much fallibility "greatness" can stand leads me to recall, and mention to Edmonds, the time Mary Pcolar praised Wilson as the Greatest Man in the World only to have him admonish her severely; it only *seemed* that way because today's portfolioed ones—presidents like Nixon—were so mediocre.

"Wilson was great and *not* great," Edmonds comments.

I ask him to explain.

"He was great of intellect, but his domestic life was deplorable. I should imagine he was a poor husband and a worse father."

I tell him about the two extremes of his domestic side that Wilson had revealed to me. The first was his tribute to Elena for the patching salve she had applied, for a quarter century, to Wilson, the father. The other was his one-word summary of an earlier marriage. In his cups and hearing Jo enthuse over the harmony that can come to a wife when she shares her husband's interests, he remembered the wife among the four with whom he had most in common, intellectually. "Hideous!" he had hissed in the huffing voice so well described by Edmonds.

Had he gone to the funeral?

"Yes. Jesse Howland called me that afternoon, just as we arrived at Northlands after driving up from Concord. We jumped back into the car and got to the Stone House barely in time. A small group gathered in the room just behind his study. It was about five o'clock. They'd brought down his old brass bed and there he was, wearing the maroon dressing gown he always liked. You know, he'd greeted the sun in that dressing gown and drinking a glass of vermouth. Looking at him for the last time, I couldn't help but think that noble head belonged in a museum with all the other great Roman heads. The minister said a short prayer, from Ecclesiastes, as Edmund had requested. Then for a few minutes you heard voices again. It was over in about ten minutes."

Edmonds remembers Wilson as "great fun—he liked fun— laugh, laugh, laugh except during the tax trouble. One time, at the height of the trouble, he told the IRS people he couldn't make an appointment with them because he was going to the White House to receive an award from President Kennedy. That baffled them."

I ask him what it was like for a writer to live through a twelve-year dry spell. He went into analysis, he says, about which he remembers nothing except that he would not have missed it for anything. "I wonder if Edmund ever saw a psychiatrist," he muses. I recall Wilson's observation on Hemingway that the Mayo Clinic—the shock treatments—had wrecked him. Edmonds hesitates, then without smiling says: "No psychiatrists for Wilson. A little like Kittredge and why he never got a Ph.D.: 'Who would there be to examine me?'"

Then, for a reason I no longer recall, I apply to Wilson the quality I never saw diminish in the decade I knew him: *seignorial*. To my joy, Walter Edmonds picks up on it. "Oh!" he exclaims, his usually even voice rising. "How he'd have loved a seignory on the Hudson!"

We have been drinking coffee and, in honor of Edmund Wilson, brownies. "Like Edmund, I have angina," he says. "There have been two heart attacks. But I can't resist cookies once in a while."

XV

Canadian Interlude: Morley Callaghan

W HO COULD TELL WHEN, marooned indefinitely two thousand miles away, I might expect to make it back Upstate? I decided one day to take Jo and Phil to see Niagara Falls from the Canadian side. An equally compelling reason, however, was to go to Toronto and see again my old friend Earle Birney, the poet from Banff. So I wrote him, mentioning the Wilson labors casually. His reply suggested an unanticipated dividend. "If you're going to write about Edmund Wilson and you're qoing to be in Toronto, maybe I can arrange for you to talk to Morley Callaghan. They were close friends, you know."

Later, long after it was too late to do anything about it, I learned that Earle had played me up with Callaghan as an American scholar who had read all his books. The truth—remedied since—was that I knew Morley Callaghan solely from *That Summer in Paris*, the superb memoir. That book contains details of a legendary boxing incident involving Ernest Hemingway that remained literary gossip until after Hemingway's biographer, Carlos Baker, and still later, Edmund Wilson, reported the story in versions that square.

Of all the mythology that eventually sank Hemingway, the story of how Callaghan, who had boxed a bit in college, was goaded into putting on the gloves with the larger and stronger man and proceeded to give the heavyweight a boxing lesson, seemed to me an authentic gesture against the perpetrator of the Code Hero. It extended fiction into life: a sort of answer from that other—that fictional—college boxer Robert Cohn to Jake Barnes for maligning him in *The Sun Also Rises*.

Now, at summer's end, I might hear from a participant the story of how the bloodied heavyweight, without grace under pressure, had urged the agile welterweight to keep hitting him, the more blood the better, so he could feel what a bull feels. As things turned out, the conversation was so lively as to resist the introduction of gossip that was already forty-five years old.

Birney is an outlander from Banff in Calgary; and Toronto, his adopted city, is like Dostoevsky's Petersburg or Wells's London. Callaghan is establishment, although that designation would have to be qualified.

They look their parts. Birney is flamboyant; the long stride, the sense I always have when I'm with him that he can fly. He wears a beret which, when it crowns a six-foot-three-inch body and Whitmanesque beard, elevates him to a kind of godhead: a presence that towers above the commonplace he has devoted a lifetime to exorcizing from his soul. I drive because, of the three of us, I alone own a car. I make a mental note to add Callaghan's name to the long list of non-driving authors I have been compiling for years: Wilson, Evelyn Waugh, Orson Welles, Ray Bradbury.

Callaghan is waiting for us on the wide porch of his house in Rosedale, a prosperous-looking residential section. Although he is past seventy, his step is sure, though in the circumscribed way a short, compact man has. I can well imagine him side-stepping or ducking under those Hemingway haymakers. He is holding a pipe as he urges Earle back into the front seat next to me while he maneuvers himself into the window seat. Earle makes the introductions. Morley Callaghan talks with the barest suggestion of something I take to be a brogue, one not discernible to Earle, he told me later, because he has known that voice for forty years as *Callaghanian*. His hair, undoubtedly reddish in youth, is now limited to a fringe toward the back. His complexion has grown blotchy with age—not a non-drinking man, I would venture. I get the sense with Callaghan that he could take the Hemingways and Fitzgeralds, the changes of literary taste, everything, in stride. His expression is open, not given to those smiles that get pasted onto a face by overuse. I feel I am being sized up without any to-do about it. I am put at ease.

Large raindrops begin pelting down as I park no more than two long blocks from Callaghan's porch. Earle had told me that Callaghan does not like to go far because his wife of a half-century, the memorable Loretto of *That Summer in Paris*, has been ill, and confined, with heart disease. Callaghan wants us to help him test out the Mirabelle Restaurant, which looks like a private club, but one more like the Vesper in my home town of Philadelphia than the Fort Schuyler in my adopted one. We are on one of Toronto's main thoroughfares, Bloor Street (#345), Greinen Square. I recall a reference to Bloor Street as the setting for the beginning conception of the mountain in *David*, Birney's long poem that is considered a contemporary classic in Canada but regrettably not well known to U.S. students.[1]

Morley Callaghan orders a Bloody Mary, Earle a Whisky Sour, and I (in honor of Edmund Wilson, I say) a *dy-kwy-ree*. Earle, who has been a vegetarian for many years, and I ordered non-meat entrees, but Callaghan asks for a small steak. I tell the waiter I want a separate check, but Earle objects. "Don't muddy things up. You're in my country now, man."

I note that in *Upstate* Edmund had reproduced a diary entry revealing that he had not actually met Morley Callaghan until 1955.

"That's true, I believe," Callaghan says, "but he was always insisting we'd met. I remember one time, around 1929, at the old Brevoort in New York. Wilson was in earnest conversation with James T. Farrell. It was for a piece on Farrell in *The New Republic*. I didn't think I ought to interrupt. Much later—it was in '55, shortly after we'd officially met—he telephoned me about *The Loved and the Lost*, which he wanted but couldn't obtain. I mailed him a copy. Ten days later I had a call from Talcottville. Edmund was very excited. Elena had read it and urged him to get to it right away—one of the best novels of the last ten years, he called it. Wilson told my son Barry that writers from all over the world were always buttonholing him to read their books but here's Morley Callaghan whose novels he'd like to read but can't get."

Callaghan relates to us an extraordinary story involving Edmund Wilson and F. Scott Fitzgerald that had just been published as a short preface to a Laurentian Library (Canadian) edition of his novel *It's Never Over* (1930).

"One of those ironic satisfactions, that are precious and often take forever to unravel, has to do with Wilson and my 'death-house masterpiece,' as Scott Fitzgerald called, not without sarcasm, *It's Never Over*. It was the book I was working on in Paris in 1929, the summer of that memoir I wrote years later. The only one I talked to about it was Fitzgerald, and the last time I saw him I went over the whole story. He was full of enthusiasm for the book. Then came the boxing match with Hemingway, with Scott as referee and timekeeper. Don't ask me to go into that again. There were exchanges of insults in our letters over that incident, and eventually Fitzgerald had to make a formal apology to me. Jump ahead to the early 1960s. Reading the letters of F. Scott Fitzgerald, my eyebrows went up. He had written to someone, 'If you think Callaghan hasn't completely blown himself up with this death-house masterpiece, just wait and see the pieces fall.' Then Edmund wrote me from Rome. He had read Scott's letter. How was it that the 'deathhouse masterpiece' was the one book of mine he hadn't read? One night, same way as in '55, he phoned from Talcottville. He said he had been unable to put the book down. Then he told me not to kid myself about Fitzgerald 'Scott would know how good a book that was.' Edmund's explanation for Scott's nasty comment was that it, like so many other unfortunate things, stemmed from his emotional involvement with Hemingway after the insults. As everyone knows, Fitzgerald regarded Edmund Wilson as his literary conscience. So it took thirty-five years, but at the end I was able to say to myself, 'Well, there you are, Scott.'"

Callaghan makes no effort to conceal such evidences of literary in-fighting. He notes dispassionately his suspicion that the man whom he met as a fellow reporter on the *Toronto Star* in the mid-twenties—the young story writer from Oak Park, Illinois, named Ernest Hemingway—had deliberately held for more than eighteen months the manuscript of Callaghan's first stories "because he didn't want me to get launched until his own *In Our Time* stories were afloat." Callaghan pauses for a moment. "I couldn't know then that Hem was going through divorce and remarriage." He is unqualified in his gratitude for Hemingway's help at the start of a career that has extended a half-century.

"My son Barry would often get down to Wellfleet to see Edmund Wilson. He attended the memorial service two summers ago. Edmund told Barry that my writings on Scott Fitzgerald's novels were the best he had ever read. But the only things I ever wrote were responses to critiques by professors who didn't know when Scott was good and when he was bad. I always admired *The Great Gatsby* but thought the last third of *Tender Is the Night* flawed. Once when Edmund said to me that he thought the two novels would stand up, I expressed my opinion. Years later he told me he'd come to agree. Fitzgerald lost focus on Dick Diver in the last third."

I ask Callaghan a question Chuck Booth had posed to Edmund Wilson twelve years ago. Would he care to comment on Faulkner's ranking of Thomas Wolfe as first in his—and Callaghan's—generation, followed by Dos Passos and Fitzgerald, with Hemingway only fourth? Callaghan does not resist the question as Wilson had. "I think a prose writer who tries always for the poetic effect is skirting danger. I confess to falling somewhat in the category of those who keep hearing echoes of other writers, especially poets, in Wolfe's prose."

Earle Birney warms to the notion that one writer could adopt the "feel" of another—perhaps unwittingly. He speaks of Malcolm Lowry, who considered himself a flawed novelist, a kind of subjective poet, as one with a way of being admiringly predatory in the using of other writers' material and even contrite about it at the same time.

"In September 1947, about six months after the publication of *Under the Volcano*, I showed Malc a letter of acceptance and a copy of my poem, 'Winter Saturday.' A few days later Lowry wrote to his friend the Irish novelist James Stern and, unknown of course to me at the time, used a line—'the town was less than its glow'— as if it were his own. I discovered this only when Lowry's *Selected Letters* appeared almost twenty years later. And I found an unpublished letter of Lowry's in the University of British Columbia collection, written later still, in which Lowry appeared to believe *I* had stolen the line from *him!*"

Callaghan has not finished his answer to the question occasioned by Faulkner's ranking. He goes on:

"Hemingway was a great descriptive writer, primarily. I

remember introducing Thomas Mann up here during the war. It was an anti-Fascist rally. Mann described, in private conversation, *A Farewell to Arms* as a perfect lyric book. I've always considered Cat Barkley as just a sofa pillow in the book. Mann thought the love-and-death stuff at the end as absolutely necessary in the lyric scheme of things." I told Callaghan about an anti-Cat Barkley paper that I'd heard the previous fall that "stopped the show" at a usually austere American literature session. The paper set out to prove that Frederic Henry was not so much enamored of Cat Barkley as he was bored by her. J. F. Kobler had called his essay "Let's Run Cat Barkley Up the Flag and See Who Salutes."

"Faulkner was a very great writer," Callaghan continues. "Especially the Faulkner that preceded his Nobel Prize speech. I've always felt that long preface to *The Bear* to be overdone."

Earle agrees. "*The Bear* just doesn't *teach* because of the preface," he says.

Callaghan believes that the Nobel Prize doomed Faulkner to being a celebrity. Despite Faulkner's passionate insistence on his privacy, the personal impact of the Nobel and the fame of the acceptance speech led to totemizing the man and to a kind of elevated prose.

What does he think of Mordecai Richler and the fame of *Duddy Kravitz*?

"I've served my apprenticeship with the novel of Jewish life. When I picked up Richler I looked for something else—a *Montrealized* difference. But it's the same tribal thing. I don't read him any more."

I note that Wilson admired James Baldwin because he could read him without always being reminded that he was black.

"Much as I admire Alfred Kazin, I can't accept his dictum that the American psyche is Jewish," Callaghan says. "That's a long shot."

"When I think of Watergate," Birney declares, "I get a combined sense, not of a Jewish psyche but of old lace-curtain conscience and American imperialism."

I engineer the conversation back to Wilson.

"Yes, of course, Edmund had enormous prejudices grimly admitted or lavishly disguised," Callaghan says.

"But many of them are grimly unadmitted and lavishly

undisguised in *O Canada*," Birney fires back. "That book pretended to talk about Canadian literature generally but showed an ignorance of any writing done west of Toronto. Whom did he talk to but his old cronies in Toronto? Did he ever go to Edmonton?"

"What, really, would he have found if he'd gone, say, to Edmonton?" Callaghan counters. "I don't believe you have to go to Edmonton to know about a writer from Edmonton. If he's any good, you can grasp him anywhere."

For the reader gratefully accustomed to expect of any subject Edmund Wilson tackled, however complex, a distillation, the reading of *O Canada* may disappoint; it does, in fact, bear out Birney. Although asserting that "I have made no attempt in what follows to do justice to everybody and everything," Wilson, in fact, writes at length about only three novelists of English Canada, none from west of Toronto: Callaghan, Hugh MacLennan (Cape Breton), and John Buell (Montreal); one poet, E. J. Pratt (Newfoundland); and seven writers of French Canada, poets Emile Nelligan ("the only really first-rate Canadian poet that I have yet read"), Hector de Saint-Denys-Garneau and Anne Hebert ("both tend to run to half-prose strophes that remind me of Paul Claudel—a writer I temperamentally so much dislike that I suppose I cannot do him justice, and so perhaps cannot do them justice."), and novelists Marie-Claire Blais ("a writer in a class by herself . . . incapable of allowing life in French Canada to appear in a genial light or seem to embody any sort of idea"), Roger Lemelin and Gabrielle Roy (seen by Wilson as "realists" whose early books "made a considerable impression . . . but the non-Canadian reader must recognize that the interest of a book in the context of a local situation may not necessarily coincide with its interest as literature seen in a larger context. Such a reader will have some difficulty in getting through these long prosaic novels"), and André Langevin, whose "somber stories have a moral interest, as well as tragic force, that make them parables of human destiny and not merely reports on the local life."

At this point, Birney turns to me: "If you had been brought up in the American West you could understand something of the sensitivities of western authors when they are ignored. In fact, Wilson's book is as silly in its prejudices as it would be if a Canadian wrote the story of American literature, leaving out everybody living west of Chicago."

"As a matter of fact," Callaghan says, "Edmund once told me that he'd grown sick of novels about the American Midwest. He'd been obliged to read so many of them—Sinclair Lewis, Sherwood Anderson, Willa Cather, Dreiser. He developed an inverted prejudice."

Birney reiterates his respect for an earlier Wilson. "I was permanently influenced by books like *To the Finland Station* and *Axel's Castle*. It's a disappointment that a man who had once been a damned good critic would write such a piece of balderdash."

I ask Callaghan how well his son knew Wilson. Barry Callaghan's eulogy in *Exile* contains the most moving description of the memorial service anyone had written.

"Barry, to my surprise, really liked Edmund. They'd hassle for hours over literary and political matters. In fact, Barry saw much more of him than I the last years. There was this about Edmund Wilson. You *were* or you *weren't*. A woman was a woman—she had womanly qualities—or she didn't. He was always with me—there's no other word—rather sweet. Always."

Earle is not so easily placated He had set up this meeting between admirers of Wilson, but the minority report had to be heard, too. "Wilson's snobbery and disdain have been harmful to me and all the other Canada writers he overlooked. He's dishonored his reputation up here."

"A curious irony," Callaghan volunteers. "His widow, Elena, was Elena Thornton. She lived for years in Montreal."

"Yes. She once was the wife of Edward Thornton, Canadian Pacific tycoon. *Snawbs*."

Birney's most pejorative word is *snob*, which comes out *snawb*, just as Wilson's was *trashy*. In an hour and a half, Callaghan reveals no equivalent vocabulary for derogation. For him Elena Mumm Thornton Wilson remains a "fabulous lady."

Callaghan and Birney fall to reminiscing. They agree that

they have known one another since the thirties. Birney was literary editor of *Canadian Forum*.

"I heard a good deal of you, Earle, during the Malcolm Lowry vogue," Callaghan says. As might be expected from a writer who is antipathetic to prose writers who try for a poetic effect, Callaghan never became sold on *Under the Volcano*. "You know I tried to read it when it came out, but I couldn't get beyond fifty pages. Years later, because of your writings, I tried again. Same problem. I once told a famous literary lady about my difficulty. 'You know,' she said, 'I can't read it either.'"

Callaghan has not once mentioned the referent for *it*, but I know that the vote on Lowry and *Volcano* is the same as that of Wilson. I had failed in all the years I knew him to persuade Wilson to read *it*, and I shall not try to persuade Callaghan now. I am relieved when the subject changes.

"Did you attend the service at Wellfleet?" This from Birney to Callaghan.

"Yes. Roger Straus phoned me and suggested I come down. As you said, Barry has written up the service and its aftermath. My most moving memory is of Renata Adler. She's a Rothschild, you know. She joined neither *The New Yorker* contingent nor those of us who knew him as family. She stood alone. After the service, she said a brief goodbye to each of us and walked off by herself into the woods nearby. A study in itself, just to watch her drawn inside herself, alone."

Finally Morley Callaghan delivers his own last words on his late friend: "He and I are persons who took in someone quickly and overall. Either that person was someone you could count on or he wasn't. Edmund knew from the start I was someone he could count on, and I knew he was someone I could count on."

XVI

Mariska

That summer, when Mary was out of a job, she became indispensable to me. She not only worked with me at Hungarian, she drove me around, typed my manuscripts and letters, and provided me with a pleasant companion who never got on my nerves. . . . She has brought up her three children so that they are much better trained than many of the children of my literary and academic friends.—Edmund Wilson

LEON EDEL, the tireless biographer of Henry James and Edmund Wilson's choice to be his literary executor, believes that the self-confident and self-assured Helen Mather Kimball Wilson—Edmund's mother—was responsible for her son's attitude toward women. "She was impregnable," Professor Edel writes. "She seemed masculine in areas in which the father tended to be feminine. . . . [She could] inspire fear."[1] Edel concludes that Wilson's ideal of womankind was an amalgam of the mysterious, elusive, independent-hence-unattainable kind, of which Edna St. Vincent Millay was prototypical, and the "democratic earthly woman." The biographer believes that in the story, "The Princess with the Golden Hair,"[2] Wilson dramatizes the conflict between an idealized version of his mother and a dance-hall girl who becomes the narrator's mistress.

In advancing age, the Upstate Wilson was strongly drawn to stable and resourceful earth-mother women. My belief is that Mary Pcolar's strong appeal stems from this attraction.[3]

By sheer coincidence, that summer of 1974, we rented an apartment on Rome's North George Street to be near Jo's married sister. I phoned Mary and was overjoyed to learn that she was managing a book-and-record shop only two blocks away on West

Dominick Street. Now, surely, I would learn something of the basis of their companionate symbiosis.

In the report that follows I have made no attempt to gloss over the initial impatience I felt at my failure to obtain the answers I had hoped for. As the summer wore on—as we both thawed out under daily exposure to one another—I began to understand that their relationship was a complex one that was not to be defined by her attractiveness and his fame.

If I may apply to her a term from the theater, Mary Pcolar is a "slow study." Highly intelligent, she is unliterary, at times almost inarticulate, incapable of giving in to the revealing digression, the flight of fancy that provides tone for an hour. Sometimes, wishing for more, I allow myself to wonder if she has ever read a novel through since her beloved *Tale of Two Cities*, which she tells me is the first book she ever read. I can easily believe her when she says she never expressed a difference of opinion with her "Mr. Wilson."

And yet . . . And yet Edmund could write in *Upstate*: "I never leave Talcottville nowadays without an uncomfortable feeling of never being able to do justice to my relation to Mary Pcolar."[4] To fathom the curious link between the West Leyden farmer's daughter and the man who had loved Edna St. Vincent Millay, married Mary McCarthy, and proposed to Anaïs Nin, I feel similarly inadequate. Morning after morning, through the early summer, I pursue, more doggedly than hopefully, our chats at the Blue Madrigal, the book-and-record shop that Mary manages for an absentee owner. She opens the store at ten daily except Sundays. We meet at eight and converse until 9:45.

I wonder, without ever speaking of it, how many times since his death, she has been asked if they slept together. In the course of our talks she reveals two such instances. Frederick Exley asked her pointblank. So did Barry Callaghan. "They'll never find out from me," she interjects at an unguarded moment. Her invariable refrain goes like this: "I never thought of him that way. He was an *old man* when I met him—the dearest man I have ever known. We were not lovers—at least not in *that* way."

At no point do I rise above conjecture, even a kind of unworthy speculation. I think uneasily of Phito Thoby-Marcelin's recollection that Edmund, regretful of getting old, had spoken of reaching the age when he could make love to no one but Elena. Mary, who for a short time taught Mohawk Airlines attendant trainees in the social graces, seems to sense my unease, *the* question hanging in the air between us. With a husband and three grown children, a family unit the frustrated *paterfamilias* in Wilson admired, Mary has every reason to be careful.[5]

One day, perhaps aware of my impatience with her rundown of one chauffeur's chore after another, she begins in a way that is unusual for her, anecdotally. For once, my attention does not wander. "Once—I can never remember years; it was the fall he came back up here for his talk on the Iroquois—we drove much farther than usual, as far as *Palmyra*.[6] Mr. Wilson was always revising his *Dead Sea Scrolls*; he was especially interested in the shrine at Palmyra. Could Joseph Smith actually have found on the side of a hill, right here in Upstate New York, new Bible scriptures that an angel from heaven gave him? Of course, Mr. Wilson thought he knew better. We would have some fun. At the Mormon information desk, he went right up to a woman missionary. 'Where are the Plates?' he asked. It was not a nice thing to do, but she was ready for such questions. 'They are in Heaven,' she answered, explaining that the angel who had 'loaned' them to Joseph Smith had taken them back. Mr. Wilson was chuckling all the way to the car.

"It was growing late by this time," she continues, "to be so far from Talcottville. There was a hotel at the place where we were dining. Mr. Wilson had consumed his usual large amount of scotch, and I had not watched myself the way I had learned to; that is, keeping several highballs behind. 'Do you think you can drive, Mary?' he asked. I did a frivolous thing. It must have been the drinks. I reached in my pocketbook for the car keys and dropped them in front of him. I laughed. 'Do *you* want to drive?' [Mary knows it is unecessary to remind me that Edmund does not drive.] 'We could stay here for the night.' Now it was Mr. Wilson's turn to laugh—mostly the scotch, I thought. I would have done whatever he wished. 'No, Mary,' he said. 'Whatever should we do? You don't play cards, and I have no new tricks to show you.'

"There, you *see*," she says, rather too emphatically. She quickly tacks on the intended moral: "Mr. Wilson knew our love could never be *that* kind. It was his way of telling me he knew."

I should describe Mary Pcolar. I get a good view as we sit in a corner of the store where we cannot be seen from Rome's main street—West Dominick—at an hour when people are driving or walking by on their way to work. I occupy a high stool of the kind she uses to reach albums that are shelved over her head. She sits slightly below me in an executive chair, swivel type. At forty-six she has assisted her natural East European blondeness since I was her teacher in that memorable journalism class in the fall of 1964. Although Wilson wrote in *Upstate* that he could not accept a tinted Mary ("She horrified me by having peroxided her hair. I told her that this was all wrong for her, it did not fit her clothes and color, and she said other people had said the same thing, and she was going to dye it back"[7]), it was not cosmetics he opposed so much as the affront of this daughter of peasants to follow fashion. In his late years, Wilson became positively Tolstoyan. He marvelled at Mary's high cheekbones—the authentic Mongol strain, he insisted. To the aging Edmund, no longer at home in urban America, Mary was like Tolstoy's mouzhik, deified, out of time and place.

The cheekbones, Mongol strain or not, are at best controversial as beauty marks. To me it is the eyes, the palest of blue—they and her extraordinary complexion—that stake her claim to beauty.

She tells me she identifies with Liza Doolittle. She knows *My Fair Lady* but has not read Shaw's play although Edmund had suggested it to her. I find myself thinking of her more in terms of Samuel Richardson's *Pamela*. I ask her if she has read it. She has not even heard of it. I tell her that Pamela Andrews also came from peasant farmers. I skim over the plot, remembering Dr. Johnson's words that anyone who reads Richardson for the story would shoot himself; that you read him for the sentiment. Mr. B. was a squire on whom Pamela was dependent if she were to avoid the fate of servant girls of the eighteenth century: concubinage or, worse, spinsterhood. I try to forge an analogy. "Now, of course, Edmund Wilson was no squire and you were no maiden, but he would like to have been master of a sort of squirearchy in Talcottville, and you were seeking, through him, to avoid the humdrum life of a clerk at Kramer's Pharmacy—$1.25 an hour."

My analogy is less effective with her than her parables are with me. She cannot see the relationship in Pamela-esque terms.

"I never felt for a moment like that," she protests. "Mr. Wilson was simply too old for me to worry about being chased." I want to add: "or chaste, either." Anything to add coloration—to *infect*—the antiseptic chats we are having.

Then one day, about a week after we had begun our Blue Madrigal meetings, *she* asks *me* a question. "Do you remember how shocked you were when almost none of the kids in the class had heard of Edmund Wilson?" I nod. "Well, Dick, I had never heard of him either. He was the rude old man who kept coming into Kramer's and demanding the *New York Times*, which he believed, by some act of God, was being put aside for him. Later that first summer, when I became, part-time, his secretary, I looked him up in *Who's Who*. Even then I wasn't convinced. It was the summer before President Kennedy's assassination—my second or third with Mr. Wilson—that I became convinced. He dictated a letter to President Kennedy, and I knew his importance went beyond all those book titles after his name. I can still recite that letter from memory: '*Dear President Kennedy: I am of course extremely appreciative of the award of the Freedom Medal. I am sorry that I shall be in Europe in September so that I shall not be able to be present at the ceremony. Yours Sincerely, Edmund Wilson.*' I looked at him, doubting my ears. 'Is that all?' I said. 'Yes, that's enough. Just send it out as is.' Then I *knew*."

We talk about *greatness* and how easily Wilson wore his. She never, in his presence, called him a great man. But once, in a letter, she allowed herself to be carried away. "He wrote that he'd had a stroke at Wellfleet the day before Christmas but that he had recovered except for the use of his right hand. He had to dictate the letter. A week or so later, from a hospital in New York, came something I had been 'spoiled' by for twelve years: his annual Valentine's Day and birthday greeting—mine's the same as Abe Lincoln's. This time a scrawled heart, pathetically lopsided, with the words, 'This is the best I can do this year, by way of a valentine and birthday greeting.'[8] So I wrote him a long letter expressing gratitude for all that he, the *world's greatest man*, had done for me. I received a short typewritten note asking that I dismiss from my mind any idea that he was what I'd said he was; that our President—Nixon—was so inferior that he made everyone else look better."

We find ourselves in agreement that the importance of that part of his life spent among us could not be gauged by quantity. Like me, she had never visited him at Wellfleet. "There was something he had to do before he died—something he could only do here in the country." Her pace slackens, she chooses her words more carefully than usual, and I begin to believe she has not gone over this matter with other interviewers.

"Up here, he began to recover his sense of being a father, a provider. That's why the income tax business, coming when it did, hit him so hard. It wasn't, *literally*, as bad as he made it out to be. But there he was—this generous guy, wanting, *needing* to be needed—and, suddenly, he owes the government thousands of dollars. It stunned him. And, besides, there was this need to *atone*."

Mary hesitates over the word, as if its very sound and connotation place us on a higher frequency. "We had twelve summers together, you know, and much of the time we did things you might not expect Edmund Wilson to enjoy. He liked hikes and, when his gout was too bad for walking, we'd go on picnics along the Sugar River. I'd bring the kids along. He watched them grow up. I think he looked on me as an all-purpose provider and what George and I have as the ideal family. The kind he had wanted but never had. He came closest with Elena, but he was already in his middle fifties when Helen was born, and old by the time she was a teenager. It was a great satisfaction to him when he convinced Rosalind that she ought to come up here to live. But they were very much alike, and they couldn't live under the same roof. He told me once that if he were taken ill up here Rosalind would take care of him but he wasn't sure that she'd really *want* to."

We talk about Rosalind whom I have never met but who, like her father, is regarded as something of a charming eccentric. Charles Helmsing and Eva and Phito Thoby-Marcelin *admire* her, but they decline to arrange a meeting with her for me. Finally, as the time nears to return to Texas, I determine to call on her. Letters didn't work; they drew nasty rebuffs. I interrupt Mary to tell her about my single encounter with Rosalind Baker Wilson.

I parked that afternoon in front of the old house, which was up for sale. A sheet of paper, the ink already fading, was tacked to the front door listing the name of an agent in Lowville. I strolled down the road toward the gray clapboard house that I knew to be occupied by Rosalind. A teenage boy, hitchhiking to Boonville, stood across the highway.

"Who lives here?" I asked the boy, knowing damn well who lived there.

"Rosalind," the boy answered.

"Is she home when the car's in the driveway?"

"Rosalind's always home. Why don't you knock? She'll answer."

So I knocked or rather bumped, there being no apparent bell. A dog barked. No answer. I was about to follow the directions that were written on a note pinned to the door—"If car's in driveway and no one answers go around to back and yell." Then a voice:

"I'm coming!" The door opened just enough so that I got a full view of the great Roman head, the searching eyes—all very much as if Edmund Wilson was facing me from the grave. I identified myself, lying: ". . . I won't mention your father's name . . ."

"This is a very bad time," the words issued forth, pleadingly. It was 1:30 in the afternoon. Her father had been dead two years. "I know you're a nice man and that your wife is lovely. My father liked you both. He talked about you. But . . . Please, I can't see you. Please, I can't."

And that, regrettably, was all.

Almost all. I ask Mary if she remembers a long letter to the editor of the weekly Boonville *Herald* from Otis Munn, a cousin of Edmund's. In *Upstate*, Wilson quotes another cousin, Helen Auger, as saying that the Munn branch of the family had "lost their education and married *peasants*." The offending cousin long deceased, Munn chides Cousin Edmund on his "helplessness," his inability to drive an automobile, his having left his income-tax filing in the hands of a dead attorney. But I remembered less that letter than Rosalind Wilson's kindly reply to the editor a week later. It provided a short course on the unreliability of diaries and letters as literary forms. "We all say things about our neighbors and relatives which are not things we would want to weigh in any final judgment," she had written. ". . . Helen Auger may have called the Munns peasants in the morning and kings in the evening."[9] It was the kind of humane assessment one always looked for from her father. I express to Mary my hope that the scurrilous things Rosalind wrote about me in letters would not be her final judgment.

Mary espouses an "elephant graveyard" theory about Edmund Wilson's death. Here, two years later, she is still convinced that he came *home* in late spring 1972 to die. One who disagrees is his widow. I show Mary a letter I had from Elena, dated about six weeks after his death. She wrote:

> he did not go there to die. It had just become a habit to go there in spring and curiously for the first time he was not looking forward to it. I was to meet him in Northampton[Massachusetts] the day after he died and the last time I spoke to him he told me he was "anxious to get back." The last note he wrote was a subscription to a magazine which is not what somebody who thinks he is dying does.

And she added, at the close: "There was very much more to his life than the time he spent there every year—sometimes only two weeks."

I read the letter aloud. Mary smiles. "Elena treasured his life with her at Wellfleet just as I treasured his life with me in Talcottville." At times like this, Mary is positively *proprietary*. No other custody of Wilson's life Upstate dare be credited. "I believe Elena is wrong about that magazine subscription being the last note. Unless I'm mistaken, the last letter was to W. H. Auden. I typed it that last evening. It began *Dear Wystan*, and it congratulated Auden on the cottage he'd been offered by Oxford University. It is an especially interesting letter, looking back, because Auden could spend his last days free from financial troubles of the kind that worried Mr. Wilson in his old age."

I ask her about the impression one gathers from Exley's account, in the March 1974 *Atlantic*, that Edmund knew their reunion, summer of 1972, would be their last. "I shan't see you again . . ." he quotes Wilson's words to Mary as if they were a valedictory. "Mr. Exley was very careful in that passage. He wrote that they were the only words I would *remember*, and he was right." "But," I persist, "wasn't Exley counting on his ambiguity to create a dramatic effect that may not have been warranted if he'd quoted Wilson fully?"

Mary shows her impatience with such questions. "Does it really make that much difference, Dick? The point is that Mr. Wilson knew he was dying, and he wanted to die in the old house.

We almost never talked about it—death, I mean—until the last year or so. 'Mary, how long can I go on this way?' he'd ask. Then he'd realize he was feeling sorry for himself. Death and taxes—always double trouble for Mr. Wilson. Then he'd brighten things up. 'Will you come to my funeral?' 'If I did, would you know I came?' 'Oh yes.' 'Then of course I'll come.'

"You professors, I guess, think of fall as the time for beginnings. But up here in Boonville you have to believe in spring. After 1960, I had even more reason to believe in May. That was the month when it would stop snowing. It was the month he'd come back to me."

Almost from the start, Mary brings his letters, neatly packed in a large box in order of receipt. There are eighty-six in all, she tells me, and Yale University is interested in buying them.[10] She lets me take them home for study, and I bring them back each morning. "Did you notice how everything began to go wrong that last winter? He suffered a stroke on Christmas Eve. I had an automobile accident not long after getting his lopsided valentine. Then he was advised to go to Florida for the winter, a place called Naples, which he detested because it was full of white-haired people, people like himself going for the sun. He wrote of attending church with Elena—church, Mr. Wilson! Then Elena was badly shaken up when another car crashed into hers and wrecked it. She had to buy a car down there. There was a hassle about her license and renewal of the insurance. You can trace Mr. Wilson's decline in these last letters." She opens the box, pulls out a slip of note paper:

Allegheny
Wed —
31st
6:46 pm
Syracuse
wheelchair
had stroke

"It's all here. They had cancelled direct flights from Boston to Utica. I would have an additional hundred miles to drive. But the wheelchair was the real shocker."

The wait in Syracuse was the worst of her life. "It was the only time Mr. Wilson was ever late. We were building up to Hurricane Agnes; his plane couldn't land. When it was finally announced, I panicked. Can you imagine wheeling Edmund Wilson to the parking lot in a downpour?" She decided to move her car close to an exit. When she returned she found him waiting nervously in his wheelchair, attended by a porter. "I spotted the floppy hat that he always wore; his raincoat folded across his knees. Mr. Wilson was always uncomfortable with anything that was casual and brisk; he hated airports. But this time I felt an urgency.

"As I came closer, I spotted the walking-stick I had first seen when, our first summer, he had taken my two girls, Susie and Janet, on a walking tour along the Sugar River. I always considered that this walking-stick, made from the handle of one of his mother's umbrellas, was 'for show.' I would never think that again. He tried to greet me in his usual way that could make 'hello' sound like something not the least bit casual. I bent over and kissed him but all the while looking for some way to keep from showing my shock at how feeble he looked. I found it in the McGovern button he wore on his lapel, not something I ever expected of one who could turn down an invitation from Kennedy. 'What's that?' I asked, touching the button. 'But of course we must all vote for McGovern!' Hearing that from him, now so tired, I wondered what chance could Nixon have."

Only so long could anything distract her from the sight of what illness had left of Edmund Wilson. Inching his way, labored step by step, breath by breath, he somehow maneuvered himself, without help, into the front seat. His letters had conveyed the Spartan essentials of a broken part or two, not the picture of a human machine sputtering to a halt. The Edmund Wilson who had once said that the center of his universe was in the center of his brain had now, finally, to come to terms with the crumbling of his *other* self, his body. Mary says none of these things. She puts it better.

"It was as if Mr. Wilson was *thawing out* in front of my eyes."

The first thing she always did, at the start of a long auto ride, would be to make him prove that he had not forgotten the nitroglycerine tablets. He would hold the bottle aloft, and they would laugh together. But nothing ever fully dispelled her fears of the *what-if?* What if he died in her car?

This time she forgot the precaution for the certainty. She would not remind him, who was so ill, of medicine. Rather she would try to evoke for him the best times: pinnacles for them, when, heading for the open road—to Rome, Utica, Lowville, Palmyra, the five miles to her farmhouse. She would give herself—all, for the duration of the journey, his. "I spoke of his favorite Upstate couple, Eva and Phito, and how they always said it wasn't spring until Edmund and Mary came to dinner and looked at the violets outside their door. At other times he would respond, as if to the prospect of adventure: 'Then we must be off!' He'd hand me the key to the house—safe-keeping—and we'd go."

But this time, half expecting him to fall asleep during the long drive from Syracuse, Mary was surprised when Edmund insisted that they follow an old custom. They would dine at his favorite Upstate restaurant, The Savoy, which after all was on the way home, a distance of about 20 miles on Route 46.

Under her vigilant glance but once again without her help, Wilson waged a barely successful battle with enfeeblement and managed to get himself seated. "I knew how badly Mr. Wilson was feeling when he had only one of our ritual drinks—the *dy-kwy-rees*, you know. During the meal he came around. Pat Destito's usual greeting, 'Dr. Livingstone, I presume?' helped." By the time they reached the old house, awaited by Rosalind at the back porch, Edmund was animated. They made plans for another night at The Savoy and, after that, to see *The Godfather*.

"I never let myself believe what we both knew. Mr. Wilson carried on as usual with his writing, I doing his correspondence although he was too weak for dictation. Things might have gone easier if he had accepted a pacemaker for his heart. I never knew anyone to prevent him from doing what he wanted to do, and nothing could make him do what he *didn't* want to do. Mr. Wilson talked about the pacemaker the same way he once spoke to me about religion. 'There'll be no begging for Absolution from me when I have one foot in the grave.' That was the way he felt about things like pacemakers. They were against nature."

He did allow a trained nurse, Mrs. Elizabeth Stabb, to attend him three hours in the morning and to come back to stay on those nights when the pain was worse than usual. Mrs. Stabb and Wilson had an easy rapport and in no time had worked out a ritualistic colloquy. She would tell him that having to charge a trained nurse's fee to attend such an exemplary and lovable character as he was made her feel a thief. "Would you take half?" Wilson would ask. Mrs. Stabb would reply, "Would you?" There was also the ominous presence of the green oxygen bottles that did not go unused. An "emergency" telephone had been placed on the card table in the downstairs front room in which Wilson worked at a window opening to the distant Adirondacks. And, of course, Rosalind was living virtually next door.

"We did make that night on the town—dinner at The Savoy, *The Godfather* afterward. He had become almost a movie-freak in his old age, but it was getting harder and harder for him to hear. Some accounts had it that *The Godfather* was the last movie he saw. Not true. We had our night the Thursday before he died—in Rome—but that Sunday, the night before he died, he attended *The French Connection* at The Stanley, in Utica, with Anne Miller, the wife of his dentist."

I tell Mary that Charles Helmsing, from his vantage at the Fort Schuyler across the street, said to me that he will never forget the sight of Wilson, propped on the arm of Anne Miller, dragging his wasted body across Genesee Street. Then a happier thought crosses my mind. Would it not have amused Edmund Wilson, increasingly out of touch with American popular culture, to know how *au courant* he had become at the very end? Didn't the last two films he saw sweep most of the Academy Awards the following spring?

On the Saturday night before the Monday morning of his death, when Mary came to do his mail for him, Wilson asked her to go to Boonville for his newspapers, some hamburger steak ("I had never heard Mr. Wilson refer to what McDonald's serves as merely *hamburger!*") and some Neapolitan ice cream for his supper ("I had to settle for black raspberry, not his favorite"). "Mr.

Wilson was on a downer. He had just heard that Mabel Hutchins' son had had an accident with his logging truck and might have to lose the use of his legs. A few years before, Mabel's husband Everett, also a trucker, had died of a stroke shortly after the strain of a long and tiresome haul. To get his mind off the troubles of his friends which made his own even more depressing, I reminded him that he had promised to return to Talcottville later that summer for our drive to see Charlotte at Potsdam." Charlotte Kretzoi, Mary explained, was a literary woman he had met in Budapest. She was then on a grant in the States studying American literature, and would be at Potsdam State in late summer. Judging from mentions in *Upstate* and in the posthumous *Letters*, she was a much severer critic than Mary of Edmund's Hungarian, a kinder Nabokov, an admirer, not a rival.

"It always cheered Mr. Wilson to be able to look ahead to dates with friends. When he said he would certainly be coming back, I wanted to hug him to me. Mr. Wilson struggled over the date we'd agreed on; then came the words Mr. Exley partly quoted, 'I shan't see you again. His last words to me were a reminder not to forget to mail the letters."

For something of how Edmund spent his last hours, I am indebted to and quote from Frederick Exley's powerful account in *Notes from a Cold Island*, pp. 167–70, which is based on facts that were provided him by Rosalind Wilson.[11] An additional impression was given by Walter D. Edmonds (see Chapter XIV).

He died a few minutes past 6:30 on the morning of Monday, June 12, the day he was to go to Wellfleet. Sunday he'd spent a happy day with his friend Glyn Morris of Lyons Falls, a Presbyterian minister who had not been an active pastor for years. Morris had forsaken the ministry for a federal job bringing culture to rural areas. They had motored through the Lewis County countryside, exchanging anecdotes, laughing together. The following morning Edmund had wakened before six and had just been asked by his nurse whether he first wanted his bed bath or his breakfast when he began to convulse. Mrs. Stabb summoned Rosalind. When she arrived in her night clothes, Wilson was seated as if about to do a job of writing and Mrs. Stabb was administering him oxygen from one of the green bottles. Rosalind then called Dr. Bob Smith in Boonville. Edmund lapsed into unconsciousness. Dr. Smith arrived just before 6:30. Edmund never regained consciousness.

At three Mrs. Wilson arrived from Wellfleet and, as Edmund had specified in his will, a brief service was held at six that evening. Only a few Talcottville friends and neighbors were invited, his dentist Ned Miller and his wife Anne, his nurse Mrs. Stabb and her husband, Mabel Hutchins and her daughter Beverly, Mary and George Pcolar, and a few others. The only literary figure present was Walter D. Edmonds, accompanied by Kay Edmonds. A few minutes past six, Rosalind opened the doors to the "long room" and said to the mourners, "I think this is all of us. We'll not wait for anyone else." Mary Pcolar was struck by how much the phrasing and even the tone resembled Edmund's. In the long room Wilson was laid out in his white iron bed—"as though he were sleeping"—dressed in his blue pajamas and maroon bathrobe. On the nightstand next to the bed Rosalind had placed Edmund's watch and his final reading, Housman's *Last Poems*. The mourners had sent or brought flowers and to these Rosalind added a bouquet of lemon lilies and bridal wreath she had picked the night before.

Save for one man who broke down, and some touch-and-go moments for Rosalind, the ceremony was very brief and very controlled. As Wilson had requested, his friend Glyn Morris read from the first chapters of Ecclesiastes ("I communed with mine own heart, saying, Lo, I am come to great estate, and have gotten more wisdom than all they that have been before me in Jerusalem; yea, my heart had great experience of wisdom and knowledge. And I gave my heart to know wisdom, and to know madness and folly: I perceived that this also is vexation of spirit. For in much wisdom is much grief: and he that increaseth knowledge increaseth sorrow") and the ninetieth Psalm ("The days of our years are threescore years and ten; and if by reason of strength they be fourscore years, yet is their strength labor and sorrow: for it is soon cut off, and we fly away. . . . So teach us to number our days, that we may apply our hearts unto wisdom"). Mrs. Wilson blessed herself in the old Russian way, Wilson's body was taken to a crematorium at Little

Falls, and Mrs. Wilson then returned his ashes to Wellfleet. There was a memorial service for Edmund on Cape Cod (see Chapter XV, where Morley Callaghan, who attended, talks about it).

At Talcottville Rosalind had now unearthed four *reginae*, those showy Ladyslipper orchids, so difficult to grow anywhere but which had responded to the rains of Hurricane Agnes. They were cherished by Edmund who refused to reveal, even to Jo, their secret growing place Upstate. Rosalind planted these at the graveside. Like her father, they blossomed in May.

Notes

Preface

1. *New York Jew* (New York: Knopf, 1979), p. 239
2. Novelist J. F. Hopkins of Orlando, Florida, author of *McEckr'n* (New York: St. Martin's, 1980). Hop and I were both born in Philadelphia, Pa., met at West Chester State College in 1940, and entered the army together in 1943.
3. "Edmund Wilson: An Appreciation," *Times Literary Supplement* (June 18, 1972).

The Home Place

1. *Upstate: Records and Recollections of Northern New York* (New York: Farrar, Straus and Giroux, 1971), p. 4.
2. "The Old Stone House," *The American Earthquake: A Documentary of the Twenties and Thirties* (New York: Doubleday, 1958), p. 496.
3. *Ibid.*, pp. 496–510.
4. "A Treatise on Tales of Horror," *A Literary Chronicle: 1920–1950* (New York: Doubleday, 1952), p. 290.
5. "The Old Stone House," pp. 509–10.
6. *Upstate*, p. 297.
7. *Ibid.*, p. 244.

I: Privilege of Rank

1. "An Interview with Edmund Wilson," *The New Yorker* (June 2, 1962), p. 118. Reprinted with a 1965 note in *The Bit Between My Teeth: A Literary Chronicle of 1950–1965* (New York: Farrar, Straus & Giroux, 1965), p. 534.

2. A review, *The Nation* 162 (March 30, 1946): 379–81.

3. In his review in *The New Republic* 114 (March 25, 1946): 418, Cowley does not specifically link *Memoirs of Hecate County* with Sherwood Anderson's book, but he does acknowledge that "all six stories . . . fit into one physical and social and moral frame."

4. "Asked [by classes at the University of Mississippi in April 1947] to rank the group who had come along and developed at about the same time he did, [Faulkner] named Wolfe, John Dos Passos, Hemingway, Willa Cather, and John Steinbeck. . . . They had all failed to achieve the dream, he said, but judged on the splendor of the failure he would rank them this way: Wolfe, Faulkner, Dos Passos, Hemingway, and Steinbeck." Joseph Blotner, *Faulkner: A Biography* (New York: Random House, 1974), II: 1232.

5. "An Almost Imaginary Interview: Hemingway in Ketchum," 29, 3 (Summer 1962): 395–405.

6. "A Pleasure, Mr. Maugham," *Nimrod* 21, 1 (Fall/Winter 1976–77): 108–22. The interview with W. Somerset Maugham, which took place at Cap Ferrat, in the south of France, the day after Labor Day, 1959, was syndicated by North American Newspaper Alliance that fall and widely published in U.S. newspapers.

7. Wilson reported at length on his one meeting with Beerbohm in an essay, "A Miscellany of Max Beerbohm," *The Bit Between My Teeth*, pp. 41–62, but does not quote Sir Max as saying that he did not like Maugham's face, only that he had never been able to caricature it although he had tried several times.

8. Reprinted as "The Apotheosis of Somerset Maugham," *Classics and Commercials: A Literary Chronicle of the Forties* (New York: Farrar, Straus, 1950), pp. 319–26.

9. Later, Edmund admitted in conversation that he had never read *Cakes and Ale*—or any of Maugham's other major novels such as *Of Human Bondage* and *The Razor's Edge*. He made a similar admission to Richard Cordell, a Maugham biographer. See Ted Morgan, *Maugham: A Biography* (New York: Simon and Schuster, 1980), p. 501. Morgan also quotes Maugham as saying of Wilson, "He's the most brilliant man you have, you know" (p. 501).

10. For evidence of her continuing regard and feeling, see Rebecca West, "The Real H. G. Wells," *London Sunday Telegraph* (June 17, 1973): 13.

11. This was one of the few times the name of Nabokov ever came up in our conversations.

12. "O Canada: An American's Notes on Canadian Culture," *The New Yorker* 40, 39 (November 14, 1964), 40 (November 21, 1964), and 41 (November

28, 1964). These three essays, with a small amount of additional material, became the book, *O Canada* (New York: Farrar, Straus and Giroux, 1965).

13. Wilson described Hemingway as an "exhibitionist," a jokester whose jokes were sneers, a ribber who always lapsed into the insulter, a humorist, though never about himself, an "insufferable" man, altogether an "improbable human being," *The New Yorker* (February 23, 1963), pp. 139–42. Mary Hemingway's reply, in which she expresses regret that Wilson did not display the kind of moral objectivity for which he commends Morley Callaghan, appeared under "Department of Further Amplification" in *The New Yorker* (March 16, 1963), p. 160.

14. *The New Yorker* (February 22, 1947), p. 97.

15. *The New Yorker* (December 13, 1961), p. 125.

16. Written from Wellfleet, dated September 14, 1971. Edmund Wilson Special Collection, Yale University.

17. The pages of *Upstate* contain many hints of the frustrated *paterfamilias* such as this one: "Elena was later to reproach me for taking more interest in [Mary] than I do my own daughters. But the sole function I can have with young people seems to come down to instructing them, and neither Rosalind nor Helen has ever shown any signs of caring to be instructed by me" (p. 284).

II: Serenade and Sendoff

1. To what he called Pasternak's "constant and skilful duplicity," Edmund added his belief that Pasternak was not always aware of the "poetic implications of his apparently realistic imagery. His poetry . . . is full of metaphors not immediately identifiable and unexpected associations of ideas, which must have gone straight to the page from the poet's mind without his having reasoned about them." "Legend and Symbol in *Doctor Zhivago*," *The Bit Between My Teeth*, pp. 471–72.

2. The song begins something like this: *Oh Mari, Oh Mari, how much sleep have I lost over you; let me sleep just one more night in your embrace . . .*

3. In rereading Edmund's *New Yorker* pieces, I found a clue: "Italian love songs: They are still singing *Oi, Mari* as they were in 1945 and as they were in 1908, when I first heard it, on a steamer of the old North German Lloyd line. It was sung by a man in the steerage" (May 21, 1966), p. 57.

4. Perhaps Edmund's foremost link to the village of Clinton. Of Grace Root he wrote in *Upstate*: "She is still going very strong in her role of salon hostess. . . . I had been writing about Kelly Prentice and talked to her about the special characteristics of the people who came from Albany, of whom she seems to me a typical representative. I have a feeling that the Albany James family must have looked and talked rather like her: clever intellectual conversation, rather old-fashioned formality" (p. 308).

5. *Henry James and H. G. Wells*, edited by Gordon Ray and Leon Edel (Urbana: University of Illinois Press, 1958).

6. A novel by Henry James, Wells wrote, "is like a church lit but without a congregation to distract you, with every light and line focused on the high altar. And

on the altar, very reverently placed, intensely there, is a dead kitten, an egg shell, a bit of string," *Boon* (Atlantic Edition) 13: 455.

7. His bitterness at what he believed was the neglect of *Memoirs of Hecate County* remains one of the few instances of repetition—even the words unchanged—that I ever heard from Edmund, surely a sign of how sensitive he was on that issue.

III: "Mr. Wilson, Were You Ever a Communist?"

1. "Reporter at Large," *The New Yorker* (November 14, 21, 28, 1964).

2. However, my book was not to be published for three years—until spring 1967—and it contains later material that I attribute to Edmund.

3. William Van O'Connor, ed. *Forms of Modern Fiction* (Minneapolis: University of Minnesota Press, 1948), pp. 9–29.

4. See Edmund Wilson, *Letters on Literature and Politics,* edited by Elena Wilson (New York: Farrar, Straus and Giroux, 1977), in correspondence with Allen Tate, March 22, 1928 (p. 145), and Arthur Schlesinger, Jr., 1964 (p. 197).

5. Introduction, *Letters on Literature and Politics,* xxv.

6. Joseph Epstein, "Edmund Wilson," editorial letter, *Times Literary Supplement* (January 13, 1978).

7. *Swinnerton: An Autobiography* (Garden City, N.Y.: Doubleday, Doran & Co., 1936), p. 198.

8. Frederick Exley, *Pages from a Cold Island* (New York: Random House, 1974), p. 154.

9. See especially Wilson's poem, "Dedication," in *The Crack-Up,* etc., by F. Scott Fitzgerald, *et al.,* edited by Edmund Wilson (New York: New Directions, 1945), and "Death of Hemingway," *Upstate,* pp. 217–18.

IV: Edmund Wilson at Seventy

1. *Upstate,* p. 251.

2. "Dickens: The Two Scrooges," *The Wound and the Bow* (London: Methuen University Paperbacks, 1961, but originally published in 1941), pp. 1–93.

3. Quoted in Doris Grumbach, *The Company She Kept* (New York: Coward-McCann, 1967), p. 120.

4. Anaïs Nin, *The Diary of Anaïs Nin* (New York: Harcourt Brace Jovanovich, 1971), p. 84. Nin's entry is fascinating on Wilson, portraying as it does a kind of D. H. Lawrence situation in which Wilson's mind-consciousness ("His was a world of power and certitudes, solidities and aggressiveness. Strength and willfulness") was pitted against her blood-consciousness ("I have more affinities with those adolescents with no surplus of flesh around their soul"). Wilson, she writes, "wanted me to help him reconstruct his life, to help him choose a couch, wanted to talk with me. But I wanted to leave [his house]." One of "those adolescents" who at twenty joined Nin's

salon presents another version. Gore Vidal writes: "At no point is she aware of having been in the presence of America's best mind. But then Wilson represents all that she hates, history, politics, literature. To her, mind and feeling must be forever at war. Thus has she systematically unbalanced both art and life," *Homage to Daniel Shays: Collected Essays 1952–1972* (New York: Random House, 1973), p. 408.

5. He closes his Talcottville diary for 1964 on a note of implicit regret that he is seeing less and less of Mary Pcolar whose boss at the Rome drug store seems "to hold before her eyes a vision of a little empire of which she would be the queen." His mood turns melancholic: "I hardly ever think about the past, my ties with the old life hardly exist any more, and my relations with the current community are now something of a nuisance and annoyance," *Upstate* (pp. 276–77).

6. Dr. Bob Smith, a man of wide and humane interests besides medicine, who will be referred to with affection by Walter D. Edmonds (Chapter XIV). In *Upstate* Edmund referred to the seizure of mid-June 1965 as "the worst attack of angina since three years ago in Cambridge" (p. 285).

7. Edmund never reopened the case—at least not with me. His notion that no "great" novel can end in the complete moral "damnation," or to use Edmund's word, in the *humiliation* of the hero, has haunted me ever since. Admittedly Theron Ware's *is* complete: intellectual and religious as well as moral. *The Damnation* is the story of an Upstate Methodist clergyman during the latter years of the nineteenth century whose moral deterioration comes about by his agonizing inability to reconcile the unquestioning sectarian faith of "innocents" like his parishioners and himself with the various shades of rationalism to which he is exposed but against which the primitive Methodism of Wesley, the only kind Theron can grasp, is powerless. Theron's moral damnation issues from his futile try at moving from the non-intellectual level of his flock to a rationalist sphere that is beyond him. He falls, rather than is saved, by illumination and knowledge. It would not have been *The Damnation* I might wish to have discussed in an effort to examine Edmund's sweeping judgment. What about Hardy's *Jude the Obscure*, certainly a novel to which many have assigned greatness, in which Jude Fawley like Theron Ware is defeated morally, intellectually, and religiously by an ill-advised attempt to move out of his determinist trap?

8. "Meetings with Max Beerbohm," *Encounter* 123 (1963): 16–22.

9. Tom later relinquished the contract.

10. Edmund was working on the first volume of his notebooks when he died. The manuscript was brought to completion as *The Twenties: From Notebooks and Diaries of the Period*, edited by Leon Edel (New York: Farrar, Straus and Giroux, 1975).

11. None of the standard sources I consulted bear out Edmund. W. H. Pritchard writes that "Mr. William Rose has uncovered the birth certificate establishing that Percy Wyndham Lewis was born on November 18, 1882, on his father's yacht, tied up near Amherst, Nova Scotia," *Wyndham Lewis* (New York: Twayne, 1968), p. 19.

12. Again none of the biographical sources I consulted even hint of the possibility. Hugh Kenner writes that Dorothy Shakespear Pound's son, "Omar Shakespear Pound, was born the following year [in 1926] . . . was brought up

by [Dorothy's mother] Olivia Shakespear in London. An English school was his purgatory. They have their story, which is not this one," *The Pound Era* (Berkeley and Los Angeles: University of California Press, 1971), pp. 388–89. Charles Norman says only that "Omar Shakespear Pound was born in the American Hospital in Paris on September 10, 1926, and registered as an American citizen, his mother being American by marriage. . . . Omar was twelve when his grandmother died. He told me that Pound, whom he had not seen since infancy, and his mother did not come to the funeral, but that Pound arrived shortly after on family business. He did not see his father again until 1945," Charles Norman, *Ezra Pound* (New York: Funk & Wagnalls, 1960), pp. 357, 399.

13. "Guide to Finnegans Wake," *The New Yorker* (August 5, 1944), pp. 54f.

V: From a Distance

1. See Edmund Wilson, *The Fruits of the MLA* (New York: A *New York Review* Book, 1968). See Chapter IX.

2. (Los Angeles: Sherburn Press, 1965), p. 210.

3. See my review, "A Specious Summing Up," *English Literature in Transition: 1880–1920* 9, 3 (1966): 172–73.

4. "My Life Is an Open Book: Confessions and Digressions of an Incurable," *Reading I've Liked* (New York: Simon and Schuster, 1941), p. xxxviii.

VI: Solvency and Settlement

1. "Being Strong: Edmund Wilson's Letters," *New York Review of Books* (October 27, 1977), p. 4.

2. The play, however, appeared only in *The New York Review of Books* as *The Lamentable Tragedy of the Duke of Palermo by Henry Chettle and William Shakespeare Now First Discovered and Transcribed by Homer R. Winslow, M.A. Hillsdale, Ph.D., Harvard, Presented by Edmund Wilson* (January 12, 1967), pp. 13–23.

3. Ted Morgan notes that Wells first met Baroness Budberg ("Mourra," neé Zakrevskaya, Maria Ignateyevna) in 1914, when she served as his interpreter. She was the mistress of Maxim Gorky during the latter's Berlin period but joined Wells when Gorky departed for Russia in 1933. She remained with Wells until his death in 1946, but would not marry him; *Maugham: A Biography*, p. 382.

4. Their long and happy marriage ended with Phito's death in 1975 at the age of seventy, a contented survivor of ten Upstate winters.

5. *Letters on Literature and Politics*, p. xxix.

6. *Upstate*, pp. 294–95.

VII: Of Flattery's Lower Forms: Conrad Aiken

1. An expanded version of my seminar paper was published as "*Ulysses*, Lowry's *Volcano*, and the *Voyage* Between: Study of an Unacknowledged Literary Kinship," *University of Toronto Quarterly* 36, 4 (July 1967): 335–52.

2. For a fuller, account of the two talks with Aiken, see my "Conrad Aiken (1889–1973): The Wages of Neglect," *Fiction International* 2 and 3 (1974), 76–80.

VIII: The Public Wilson

1. "Reporter at Large: On the Eve," *The New Yorker* (August 19, 1967), pp. 38–40.

2. Edmund, for all the years I knew him, was always doing work-in-progress on the Dead Sea scrolls. Sherman Paul believes that, for Wilson, "the importance of the Dead Sea scrolls—their discovery is the only major event of the atomic age that Wilson has chosen to report in detail—lies in the fact that they force one to ponder the origins of Christianity and to entertain the provocative idea that man himself evolved it," *Edmund Wilson* (Carbondale: Southern Illinois University Press, 1965), p. 185. There were three major editions. The first, *The Scrolls from the Dead Sea* (New York: Oxford University Press, 1955), was the product of Wilson's journey to the Holy Land in 1954; the second, *The Dead Sea Scrolls, 1947–1969* (Oxford, 1969), revised and expanded the original and again was the fruit of his research into newly found manuscripts as well as additional material on old ones; the third, published posthumously, *Israel and the Dead Sea Scrolls* (New York: Farrar, Straus and Giroux, 1978), brings together in one volume all of Wilson's writings on Israel and the Holy Lands. Edmund wrote that he could not be considered a Semitic scholar and likened his endeavors to those of Hemingway in relation to bull-fighting—"also an occupation which requires thorough training, strict self-discipline, and a willingness to take certain risks," *Scrolls* (1978), p. 235.

3. "Reporter at Large: On the Eve," *The New Yorker* (August 19, 1967), p. 69.

4. *Ibid.*, p. 70.

5. *Ibid.*, pp. 70, 72.

6. E. J. Kahn, Jr., *About THE NEW YORKER and Me: A Sentimental Journey* (New York: Putnam's, 1979), p. 296.

7. *Upstate*, p. 316.

8. Judging from his discussion in *Upstate* (pp. 314–15), Edmund's interest in Harold Frederic was fueled by a spirit of competition. Lafe Todd, holder of a chair of Rhetoric and Oratory at Hamilton College, had discovered Alexander Bryan Johnson (1783–1867), a Utican who had tried his hand, unsuccessfully, at

fiction but who wrote with more distinction early studies in semantics. There was to be, almost concurrently with the Frederic symposium at Utica College, two days of tribute to Johnson at the Munson-Williams-Proctor Institute. "We are running Harold Frederic as most distinguished Utica intellectual against A. B. Johnson," Edmund noted, not without pride.

9. "Two Neglected American Novelists," *The New Yorker* (May 23, 1970), pp. 112–16, and (June 6, 1970), pp. 112–14.

10. Professor Mark Hillegas, who taught the first course in science fiction (at Colgate in the early 1960s), notes that Kagarlitski's edition of Wells's works, published in 1964, was printed in 350,000 copies. *The Future as Nightmare: H. G. Wells and the Anti-Utopians* (New York: Oxford University Press, 1967), p. 189n.

11. Costa, *H. G. Wells* (New York: Twayne, 1967), pp. 158–59.

12. Costa, "Conrad Aiken (1889–1973): The Wages of Neglect," *Fiction International* 2 and 3 (1974): 77.

13. However, in *Upstate* (p. 222), Edmund observes that getting older, for a writer, does not give self-confidence. He sometimes got up at 4 o'clock in the morning to read old reviews of his books.

14. Principally "Lowry/Aiken Symbiosis," *The Nation* (June 26, 1967): 823–26.

IX: Pastoral and Polemic

1. Levin, "Edmund Wilson's Letters," *op. cit.*, 3.

2. *Upstate*, pp. 297–98.

3. *Ibid.*, pp. 321–22, 327.

4. "Living for Literature," *Times Literary Supplement* (November 25, 1977), p. 1372.

5. "Mr. Wilson and the Cold War," *Commonweal* (January 10, 1964), pp. 434–35.

6. *Edmund Wilson* (New York: Twayne, 1970), p. 27.

7. *The Fruits of the MLA*, p. 7. However, in December 1979, the sort of readable edition visioned by Edmund was announced under the combined sponsorship of the National Endowment for the Humanities and the Ford Foundation. The compact, hardbound editions of America's great books will carry the general title, Literary Classics of the United States, Daniel Aaron, Harvard University, president.

8. To deal adequately with Edmund's broadside and the able reply to it (*Professional Standards and American Editions: A Response to Edmund Wilson*, Modern Language Association, 1969) would require an examination of literary issues that are far too complex for this informal memoir. As in other matters, Wilson's and the academic scholar's interests and goals bear little relationship. Wilson's desire was for attractive volumes with excellent texts, available at moderate prices to the general reader; the American literature scholar's is for texts that are complete and correct enough for use by the advanced student. See John H. Fisher,

"The MLA Editions of Major American Authors," for a reasoned and temperate presentation of the problems. It is contained in the MLA pamphlet, above, which can be obtained from Materials Center, MLA, 62 Fifth Avenue, New York 10011 for $1.25.

9. "Edmund Wilson," *The New Yorker* (January 2, 1978): 59.

10. *Experiment in Autobiography: Discoveries and Conclusions of a Very Ordinary Brain* (New York: Macmillan, 1934).

11. Richard Hauer Costa, "The Epistolary Monitor in *Pamela*," *Modern Language Quarterly* 31, 1 (March 1970): 38–47.

12. *Apologies to the Iroquois* (essays), with a study of "The Mohawks in High Steel," by Joseph Mitchell (New York: Farrar, Straus and Cudahy, 1960).

X: A Woman's View

1. Of Charles Helmsing, Edmund wrote in *Upstate*: "The new manager [of the Fort Schuyler Club] is unexpectedly a cultivated and very agreeable man, part Russian and part Swedish, very much, I think, a Baltic type, who has lived a good deal in France and to whom I can talk about books" (p. 329).

2. The Boston Store closed down in 1977.

3. *Twenty Letters to a Friend*. Translated by Priscilla Johnson McMillan (New York: Harper, 1967).

4. *Only One Year*. Translated by Paul Chavchevadze (New York: Harper, 1969).

5. "Shadows of Popocatepetl," *Quartet* 54–55 (Spring–Summer 1976): 35–44.

XI: The Farewell Years

1. Of Dr. Edgar Miller of Lowville, Edmund wrote, "I was astonished to find dentists [in Lowville] so well equipped and staffed as he and his brothers are. He did a lot of arduous work on my lower jaw, even drilling a hole in the jawbone, and has provided me with a bridge which stays in and with which I can effectively chew. . . . Is also well-informed and intelligent. . . . The family came originally from Talcottville, and there are Millers in the cemetery on the hill," *Upstate* (p. 341).

2. *Ernest Hemingway: A Life* (New York: Scribner's, 1969).

3. *Ernest Hemingway: A Reassessment* (State College: Pennsylvania State University Press, 1966).

4. With Hoyt C. Franchere, *Harold Frederic* (New York: Twayne), 1961.

5. Gretchen Crosten was a member by marriage of one of Edmund's favorite Boonville families.

6. Birney and Wilson never met—and possibly, just as well. Earle took it

as an affront that *O Canada* takes no note of any writers who were not based in Eastern Canada. For a full discussion of this issue, see Chapter XV.

7. "Malcolm Lowry and the Addictions of an Era," *University of Windsor Review* 5, 2 (Spring 1970): 1–10.

8. "The Screw Turns on Mr. James," *The Nation* 187 (August 16, 1958): 76–77.

9. "The Author at Sixty," *A Piece of My Mind* (New York: Farrar, Straus and Cudahy, 1956), p. 239.

XII. The Seignorial Stance

1. I had asked him, for an article I was writing on the suicide of actor George Sanders, the name of the persistent Italian photographers who harrass film stars and other celebrities at the Rome airport. Later I thought of it: *paparazzi*.

2. This unfortunately, was not true. For an account of Edmund's last days, see Chapter XVII.

Afterwords

1. Sheed, *New York Times Book Review* (July 2, 1972), p. 2, 16; Connolly, "Edmund Wilson: An Appreciation," *Times Literary Supplement*, June 18, 1972; Toynbee, *London Observer* (June 18, 1972), p. 33.

2. Levin, "The Last American Man of Letters," *Times Literary Supplement* (October 11, 1974), pp. 1128–30; Exley, "Good-Bye, Edmund Wilson," *The Atlantic* 233, 3 (March 1974): 75–83.

3. "Edmund Wilson," *Exile* 1, 2 (1972): 107–10.

4. Dalma H. Brunauer, *Prairie Schooner* (Winter 1976): 343–52.

5. Wilson, *Night Thoughts* (New York: Farrar, Straus and Cudahy, 1961), p. 217.

XIII: Double Meanings

1. Exley, "Good-bye, Edmund Wilson," p. 77. See Chapter XVI for Mary Pcolar's impressions of her long friendship with Edmund.

2. (New York: Random House, 1975), pp. 135–80.

XIV: Writers and Neighbors: Walter D. Edmonds

1. Few, even among the many enthusiasts over *Patriotic Gore*, have found anything to admire in it. The Introduction, misanthropic, uncompromisingly critical of the course of American history, is a "crude distillation of the politics of Wilson's

later years. . . . cut-rate Hobbesianism which *Patriotic Gore* heroically refutes. . . . Literature, fittingly in his career, triumphs over politics," said Joseph Epstein in "Living for Literature," p. 1372.

XV: Canadian Interlude: Morley Callaghan

1. Earle Birney, *The Cow Jumped Over the Moon* (Toronto: Holt, Rinehart & Winston of Canada, 1972), p. 32.

XVI: Mariska

1. Leon Edel, "A Portrait of Edmund Wilson," in *Edmund Wilson, The Twenties* (New York: Farrar, Straus & Giroux, 1975), p. xxvi.

2. See *Memoirs of Hecate County*.

·3. Edmund reinforces this impression throughout those parts of *Upstate* that are devoted to Mary, especially pp. 214–17.

4. *Upstate*, p. 284.

5. Edmund did not live to see the marriage he admired terminate in divorce in 1975. Since 1978 she has been Mrs. John J. Spitzer, Rome.

6. This was in fall 1968, between September 27 and October 20 (*Upstate*, pp. 328–29).

7. *Upstate*, p. 280.

8. More typical of Edmund's valentine cards to Mary was one dated February 4, 1966, containing a picture of a strawberry sundae and these versified words: *Such precious things are set apart/ In memory's corner of my heart/ JUST FOR YOU,/ MY Valentine and Darling, too!* To which Edmund had added "And I should like to eat you someday/ Because you are a great big Sunday [sic]." *Sunday* for *sundae* was the only example of a misspelling I had ever seen with Edmund, and in this instance it may have heen intentional.

9. Otis Munn's letter ("My Answer to [Edmund Wilson's] Talcottville Diary"), *Boonville Herald* (October 15, 1971), pp. 2–3, 10; Rosalind Wilson's reply ("Two Answers to Otis Munn's Letter"), *Boonville Herald* (October 22, 1971), p. 2.

10. Mary sold her letters two years after our chats—in 1976—to the Beinecke Library, Yale University, for $1,200 (letter to me, November 10, 1977).

11. As I explained earlier in this chapter, Rosalind Wilson declined to give me an interview. Without Exley's *Pages from a Cold Island* (Random House, 1975) and his earlier memoir, "Good-bye, Edmund Wilson," *The Atlantic* (March 1974), I would have been without a valuable resource in reconstructing Edmund's last days. Exley talked to Mary Pcolar three weeks after Edmund's death in the summer of 1972. It was inevitable that my chats with her two years later would cover some of the same territory. Except for the account of Edmund's final hours, where I have followed Exley's words closely, my contexts are different from Exley's. I highly recommend the Edmund Wilson chapters (8–11) of his book.

Index

EDMUND WILSON

was composed in 11-point Caledonia on Mergenthaler Linotron 202
and leaded two points, with display type in Deepdene,
by Eastern Graphics Photocomposition;
printed on Warren acid-free 50-pound Antique Cream paper,
Smythe-sewn, and bound over boards in Columbia Bayside Linen
by Maple-Vail Book Manufacturing Group, Inc.;
and published by

SYRACUSE UNIVERSITY PRESS
SYRACUSE, NEW YORK 13210